SUPERNATURAL SAINTS

A SCHOOL OF MINISTRY
FROM THE SAINTS

SUPERNATURAL
SAINTS

A SCHOOL OF MINISTRY
FROM THE SAINTS

PATRICK REIS

FOREWORD BY
FR. MATHIAS THELEN

Published by *Encounter Ministries*
730 Rickett Rd., Brighton, MI 48116

Printed and bound in the United States of America

ISBN- 9798354218226

Cover image ©2022 Encounter Ministries
Cover and layout by Jessica Morehead

 Imprimatur:
Printed with Ecclesiastical Permission.
Most Reverend Earl Boyea. August 14, 2022
Lansing, Michigan

Encounter Ministries exists to unleash the transforming power of the Holy Spirit into the world. www.encounterministries.us.

Endorsements

"The saints are often seen as our heroes of faith. But the stories of their lives and supernatural ministries have sometimes seemed like folk lore, and beyond the experience of us everyday believers. Patrick closes the gap between their ministry and our experience, helps us to understand their spiritual practices, and encourages us that we too can be powerful instruments of Jesus in the world. God always raises up saints to shine like lights in the world in critical moments of history. May this book equip and activate you to be a source of hope in this suffering world."

BISHOP DAVID O'CONNELL
Auxiliary Bishop of Los Angeles

"I thought I knew these saints, but Patrick Reis draws out lessons from their lives that are new, amazing, eye-opening, practical, and exactly what is needed for the Church's mission today. I find myself deeply challenged and inspired by this book."

DR. MARY HEALY S.T.D.
Professor of Scripture at Sacred Heart Major
Seminary in Detroit, bestselling author,
and international speaker

"Patrick Reis has written an important and timely book by giving us a rare look into the ministry habits and strategies of six of our most beloved saints. Supernatural Saints makes a genuine contribution to "equipping the saints for ministry" in our day by harvesting important ministry lessons from these saints who not only model for us the life of holiness and heroic virtue, but also teach us how to walk in the supernatural."

PETER HERBECK
Author, television host, and
Vice President, Renewal Ministries

"Patrick Reis has provided a treasure for us. On the one hand he brings down some of the most fantastical saints and saint stories and helps us understand them and how they could have taken place earlier today. On the other hand, he raises up our hearts and minds and helps us imagine how we could be more like them. This book is inspiring, practical, accessible, and enjoyable. It will make you want to be more like the saints and give you practical steps for growth in that direction."

FR. BONIFACE HICKS
Author and Director of Spiritual Formation
Saint Vincent Seminary, Latrobe, PA

Dedication

For my wife, Emily Reis, who inspired this project and whose love and friendship has made all my ministry possible.

FOREWORD

The Church is in trouble. Unbelief is on the rise and Christians are falling away from the faith at an alarming rate. Due to factors both in and beyond our control, much of the Church in the West is in rapid decline and suffering a crisis of faith. Fortunately, the implications of the current demographic shifts have served to reinforce our urgent need to return to God, not to human thinking, for a solution to our plight. I sincerely believe that as the Lord purifies his Church in this period of our history, we are becoming a more humble Church that is less worldly and more willing to turn to the Holy Spirit for inspiration, guidance and grace for mission.

But not all of the Church is in decline. We only need to look at what God is doing in the global south, where a "renewalist" form of Christianity, which actually exists in the West in parts, is still growing at explosive rates. The brand of Christianity that is still growing is deeply rooted in a biblical worldview, believes in the gifts of the Spirit, expects God to intervene in miraculous ways, and is committed to personal evangelization. The growth and missionary activity of renewalist Christianity is made possible by the fact that the Lord is indeed performing signs and wonders just as he did in the Acts of the Apostles and other ages of Church history in which missionary activity was strong. Where the Holy Spirit is unleashed in the Church, the Church becomes able to make disciples of nations again.

I met Patrick Reis in my first year as a priest at a small conference on deliverance ministry. Like others our age, we both had profound encounters with Jesus in Eucharistic Adoration through the ministry of Franciscan University in Steubenville, OH. We wanted to share the gospel and help the Church come alive but we came to the realization that we needed more of him for that purpose. Convinced that Jesus didn't suffer and die for a lifeless and powerless Church incapable of mediating the power of the gospel to the next generation, we decided to seek what the Lord might want to do through us for his Church.

We came to believe that it is precisely when we take seriously the gift of the Holy Spirit, the Lord and Giver of Life, and learn his ways, that the Church will be renewed. We co-founded Encounter Ministries to partner with God in unleashing the transforming power of the Holy Spirit in the world. We know many are hesitant about an increased role of the Holy Spirit in the Church on account of some confusion and erroneous pastoral practices that came to light in the charismatic renewal, which otherwise has been a tremendous gift to the Church. Nevertheless, throughout the history of the Church, ordinary lay men and women and the saints experienced the Holy Spirit's intervention in their personal lives and in their apostolates not unlike what we're witnessing today in renewalist Christianity. We're convinced that God is renewing our faith in the role the Holy Spirit plays in our pursuit of holiness and in evangelization.

For as long as I've known him, I've admired Patrick both for his radical commitment to personal holiness as a husband and a father and his willingness to run as fast (and far) as he can with the torch of the gospel. What God is doing in Patrick–his teaching, writing and leadership–is marvelous and I count it a privilege to run with him as his friend. In Supernatural Saints, my friend digs deep into the lives of six canonized saints and draws out inspiring stories and practical nuggets of wisdom on how to cooperate with the Holy Spirit.

This book is not just incredibly insightful; it is yet another confirmation of what the Holy Spirit is doing today to renew the Church. The kinds of experiences of the Holy Spirit that might seem strange to Christians not familiar with the renewalist brand of Christianity are, in fact, found in the lives of the saints, whom the Church puts forward for us as models for holiness and mission. What would happen today if God granted the whole Church a new Pentecost? All aspects of Church, family and civic life would be renewed and the faith would be much more compelling to the world. Disciples of Jesus would once again be marked by a joyful and unshakable faith that Jesus Christ, our Lord, is truly alive, and pursue a radical holiness capable of enduring the suffering of all kinds of persecution. Disciples would also once again experience the Spirit's inspiration and boldness in the preaching of the gospel to the world around them. Evangelization would return to the center of the Church's life, and the Spirit's gifts would once more empower the Church to demonstrate the truth of the gospel through various signs, wonders, and miracles as in the first Pentecost. What would it be like to be a part of such a renewal?

Open your eyes. It's here.

FR. MATHIAS THELEN, STL
President and Co-Founder
Encounter Ministries

TABLE OF CONTENTS

CHAPTER ONE

A SCHOOL OF MINISTRY

I have some really good news to share with you!

God, the creator of the universe, is deeply in love with you and has an amazing plan for your life!

God's plans and purposes are greater than any plan you could pursue on your own.

God is for you! He is not against you! He wants to be part of your life and help you overcome the challenges that you face right now.

God is not the author of the problems in your life; He is the source of the solutions that will bring good out of any situation.

God understands the shame you feel from all the mistakes you've made. He sent his Son Jesus into the world to show you what love looks like and what life can be in a full relationship with God.

Through Jesus, you can be set free from the effects of your sin and experience a new life to the fullest!

Do you want to invite Jesus into your life?

If you're reading this book, there is a good chance that you already believe this good news and are already united to Christ. Unfortunately, the world has become increasingly skeptical of this message. At this point in history, the world has been responding to this invitation with a resolute "No, thank you!"

The world tells us, 'We've heard your story, we know all about your morality and religion, but...'

- how do we know this God stuff is true?
- how can we be sure that there is forgiveness and real happiness in Jesus?
- with so many religions and belief systems out there, how do we know this one is the real one?
- where is the proof, the evidence?

As this kind of skepticism, doubt, and unbelief increase concerning the Gospel, how is the Church supposed to respond?

HOW JESUS ADVANCED THE KINGDOM

How can you know whether the basic claims of the Gospel are true?

When I have the opportunity to preach to Church groups, I often ask the audience this question. Almost all the responses people propose come in some form of explanation or persuasive argument for why they believe the Gospel message is reasonable and makes sense. We could talk all day about the Church's best response to the doubt and unbelief of the world. Instead, I propose that we respond in the way that Jesus did.

Early in his ministry, Jesus was in Capernaum preaching. A large crowd gathered at the house he was in; it was so crowded that no one else could enter and get close to Jesus. Four desperate men were carrying their paralyzed friend; they wanted to get him close to Jesus. They wanted him to be healed. They carried him onto the roof, opened that roof, and lowered their friend down into the home, right next to Jesus. Jesus looked at their paralyzed friend and said to him, "My son, your sins are forgiven" (Mark 2:5).

How does the crowd around Jesus respond to this claim? "Why does this man speak this way? He is blaspheming" (Mark 2:7). Doubt, skepticism, and unbelief.

How does Jesus respond?

> "Which is easier, to say to the paralytic, 'Your sins are forgiven,' or to say, 'Rise, pick up your mat and walk'? But that you may know that the Son of Man has authority to forgive sins on earth" — he said to the paralytic, "I say to you, rise, pick up your mat, and go home." He rose, picked up his mat at once, and went away in the

sight of everyone. They were all astounded and glorified God, saying, "We have never seen anything like this." (Mark 2:9-12)

Jesus' response to the doubt and unbelief of the world around him about his ability to forgive sins was a supernatural demonstration.

As we read through the New Testament, we see that Jesus was continually "proclaiming the Gospel of God" (Mark 1:14). While he proclaimed the Gospel, he always accompanied it with supernatural signs, wonders, miracles, and healings. He was modeling a standard of ministry.

The first title Jesus' disciples used for him was "Rabbi," which literally means "teacher." Jesus was essentially leading his disciples in a school of ministry. He was not content to have them simply watch him advance the kingdom. As he taught them, he expected them eventually to do exactly what he did.

In Matthew 10:1 Jesus imparts to the disciples "authority over unclean spirits to drive them out and to cure every disease and every illness." He then sends them out on mission, saying, "Do not go into pagan territory or enter a Samaritan town. Go rather to the lost sheep of the house of Israel. As you go, make this proclamation: 'The kingdom of heaven is at hand.' Cure the sick, raise the dead, cleanse lepers, drive out demons" (Matthew 10: 5-8).

Do you see the connection here? Jesus commanded the disciples to preach the Gospel and then to demonstrate the message with supernatural signs. He had already modeled this for them. His ministry reflected the goodness of the Father. It made present the prayer he taught the disciples: "Your kingdom come, your will be done, on earth as in heaven" (Matthew 6:10). There is no disease, death, or demons in heaven. Whenever Jesus healed the sick, raised the dead, or cast out demons, he gave a supernatural sign to everyone around him of what his kingdom is like.

In Luke 10, the number increased to seventy. Jesus commanded them to do the same thing (see Luke 10:1-12). Following this mission of preaching and supernatural demonstration, "The seventy returned rejoicing, and said, 'Lord, even the demons are subject to us because of your name!'" (Luke 10:17). Their joyful response was incredible, and Jesus' response was even more profound:

At that very moment he rejoiced [in] the holy Spirit and said,

> "I give you praise, Father, Lord of heaven and earth, for although you have hidden these things from the wise and the learned you have revealed them to the childlike." (Luke 10:21)

This is the one time Scripture records that Jesus rejoiced in the Holy Spirit! The object of Jesus' joy was witnessing his disciples becoming more like him and doing what he did.

Jesus is the ultimate standard of all life and ministry. His desire is that "whoever believes in me will do the works that I do, and will do greater ones than these, because I am going to the Father" (John 14:12).

Do you see the pattern here? Over and over again, Jesus sets the expectation that his disciples follow after him in every way and do the same kind of ministry that he does. Before ascending into heaven after his resurrection, he gave a commission to his disciples, including us:

> "Go into the whole world and proclaim the gospel to every creature. Whoever believes and is baptized will

be saved; whoever does not believe will be condemned. These signs will accompany those who believe: in my name they will drive out demons, they will speak new languages. They will pick up serpents [with their hands], and if they drink any deadly thing, it will not harm them. They will lay hands on the sick, and they will recover."

So, then the Lord Jesus, after he spoke to them, was taken up into heaven and took his seat at the right hand of God. But they went forth and preached everywhere, while the Lord worked with them and confirmed the word through accompanying signs. (Mark 16:15-20)

HOW THE EARLY CHURCH ADVANCED THE KINGDOM

What followed Jesus' time on earth is recounted in the Book of Acts. How exactly did the early disciples advance the kingdom of God? They did exactly what Jesus commanded them to do: they preached the Gospel and demonstrated it through supernatural ministry.[1]

For example, after Pentecost the disciples experienced persecution. Peter and John were seized by the religious leaders after preaching the Gospel and healing a paralyzed man (see Acts 3). Upon their release, they continued to fulfill their commission by asking for more power:

"And now, Lord, take note of their threats, and enable your servants to speak your word with all boldness, as you stretch forth your hand to heal, and signs and wonders are done through the name of your holy servant Jesus." As they prayed, the place where they were gathered shook, and they were all filled with the

10

holy Spirit and continued to speak the word of God with boldness. (Acts 4:29-31)

This prayer of the apostles shows how the early Church advanced the kingdom. They preached with boldness and prayed for supernatural signs to confirm the Gospel message. We shouldn't be surprised by their prayer. This is exactly what Jesus did and commanded them to do.

One of the best illustrations of this comes in Acts 8, when Philip went and evangelized the Samaritans. The Samaritans operated under a different theological system than the Jews, and there had been generations of division between these two people groups. How did Philip break through this barrier to evangelize them?

> With one accord, the crowds paid attention to what was said by Philip when they heard it and saw the signs he was doing. For unclean spirits, crying out in a loud voice, came out of many possessed people, and many paralyzed and crippled people were cured. (Acts 8:6)

It was the supernatural demonstration of healing and deliverance from demonic oppression that got people's attention and opened them to receive the Gospel.

Supernatural signs, wonders, miracles, and healings all communicate the power of God, confirming the message of the Gospel. St. Paul carried the Gospel to the nations and saw the most success of any of the early missionaries. How did he bear such amazing fruit? Paul tells us:

> I will not dare to speak of anything except what Christ has accomplished through me to lead the Gentiles to obedience by word and deed, by the power of signs and

wonders, by the power of the Spirit of God. (Romans 15:18-19)

Similarly, Paul explained how he brought the Corinthian Church to faith in Jesus:

> I resolved to know nothing while I was with you except Jesus Christ, and him crucified. I came to you in weakness and fear and much trembling, and my message and my proclamation were not with persuasive words of wisdom, but with a demonstration of spirit and power, so that your faith might rest not on human wisdom but on the power of God. (1 Corinthians 2:2-5).

In both explanations, St. Paul witnesses to the combination of the bold proclamation of the Gospel and the demonstration of supernatural signs. St. Paul knew that the gifts of the Holy Spirit enable us to demonstrate and confirm the Gospel message. After teaching the Corinthians about the spiritual gifts, he instructed them to "pursue love and earnestly desire the spiritual gifts" (1 Corinthians 14:1).

Paul shows us two things here. First, he instructs us to earnestly desire the spiritual gifts, because he knows that God earnestly wants to give them to us. Second, he points out that the Church cannot demonstrate the truth of the Gospel without the power of the Holy Spirit and His gifts.

HOW ARE WE ADVANCING THE KINGDOM?

Jesus preached the Gospel and demonstrated it through supernatural signs, wonders, miracles, and healings.

The apostles and the early Church did this as well, with great effect.

Growing up as I did in the late twentieth century, my experience of Catholic Christianity did not include supernatural demonstration. I believe I'm not alone in this. The early Church did what Jesus did and saw tremendous fruit; our generation has witnessed the opposite. Instead of gathering together and praying for an outpouring of boldness and supernatural signs, we have essentially become managers of Church decline. We have fallen into a maintenance mode of Christianity, trying to conserve what we have.

In many parts of the Church, the power of the Holy Spirit and His charisms have been marginalized. At best the charismatic dimension of the Church has been relegated to a fringe movement; at worst, it has been seen as an optional and strange spirituality or judged to be an enemy of sacramental grace and personal holiness.

The result of the marginalization of the power of the Holy Spirit and His gifts is a Church that appears weak in demonstrating the truth of the Gospel. In the absence of a Church boldly proclaiming the Gospel and seeking to

> JESUS CHRIST DID NOT DIE FOR A POWERLESS CHURCH!

demonstrate its saving truth, souls continue to leave the Church, and countless others are not reached. The most unfortunate part of this present situation is the overwhelming feeling of powerlessness: the thought that we can do nothing to stop the trend of Church decline.

But Jesus Christ did not die for a powerless Church!

THE ENCOUNTER SCHOOL OF MINISTRY

Fr. Mathias Thelen and I have experienced a calling from God to establish a school of ministry, defined by the following mission:

> Drawing from the richness of our Catholic heritage, we seek to teach, equip, and activate disciples to demonstrate the love of God through the power of the Holy Spirit in their spheres of influence.

Fr. Mathias loves to say that although signs, wonders, miracles, and healings are not the complete Gospel, the Gospel is not complete without them. The Encounter School of Ministry provides an atmosphere of faith for students to grow in the life, the power, and the gifts of the Holy Spirit and to cultivate a lifestyle based on Jesus' promise, "Whoever believes in me will do the works that I do, and will do greater ones than these" (John 14:12).

The Encounter School meets on a weekly basis over two academic years, covering eight quarters of content. Students not only receive teaching that is orthodox (right belief) but also have opportunities to cultivate orthopraxis (right practice). Each teaching session ends with the students putting into practice the ministry subject they were just learning about. All of this happens in an environment in which students can take risks; it's safe for them to make mistakes, from which they can receive guidance, learn, and mature in their ministry. We believe that all fruitful ministry flows out of intimacy with God and a full life in the Holy Spirit. In the school we are passionate about pursuing the full life in the Holy Spirit. From that place, students are activated to demonstrate the love of God through the power of the Holy Spirit.

Some of our students already have undergraduate and graduate degrees in theology. We often hear reports from them that, although they previously received a lot of theological formation, they were never instructed in how to pray with others and operate in the spiritual gifts, to advance the kingdom of God.

> WE BELIEVE THAT ALL FRUITFUL MINISTRY FLOWS OUT OF INTIMACY WITH GOD AND A FULL LIFE IN THE HOLY SPIRIT.

We believe that wherever our students have influence, they have a mission. Most people do not need to leave their world behind to go on mission. Instead, they need to cultivate a powerful lifestyle in the Holy Spirit by which they see their relationships–within a family, neighborhood, parish, or workplace–as their mission territory.

Our desire was never to build a big ministry; it was only to build big people. Through the Encounter School, we have seen ordinary, faithful Christians equipped and activated to demonstrate the love of God through the power of the Holy Spirit in their spheres of influence. Since our launch of the Encounter School, thousands of students have gone through the school and experienced transformations that have impacted their families, parishes, workplaces, and cities.

THE DISCONNECT AND THE RECONNECT

The Encounter School has grown from one campus, at our home in Brighton, Michigan, to over twenty campuses in five nations, with online teaching available in multiple languages. A team of five Catholic seminary and university professors has reviewed the school curriculum to ensure that it is completely free from any doctrinal or moral error.[2] Over twenty bishops have reviewed and approved the Encounter School of Ministry. We have experienced incredible support from the Catholic Church.

Yet as our school grew and our mission gained greater influence, Fr. Mathias and I started receiving significant pushback from some Catholics. At the heart of the opposition to our school was an assumption about the proper role and history of supernatural ministry in the Church. Although most faithful Christians believe that the supernatural dimension was certainly present in the life of Jesus, the lives of the apostles, and the life of the early Church, they see a big gap between those first years of Christianity and their experiences as modern-day believers.

A prevailing belief is that signs, wonders, and miracles were uncommon in later Church history. The thought is that these manifestations were perhaps not needed as time went on and so faded in prominence. There is an apparent disconnect between the Church portrayed in the Book of Acts and the Church that many see today. As reports of supernatural signs arise, many faithful Christians are asking, Is this stuff real? Didn't this fade away from the life of the Church?

The answer is NO! The supernatural dimension of the Church did not stop!

The truth is that over the past two thousand years, God has not stopped raising up holy men and women who experienced life-changing, personal encounters with Jesus. These men and women have been filled with the Holy Spirit! They pursued and walked in the gifts of the Holy Spirit; they cultivated lifestyles that demonstrated the supernatural power and love of God, to advance the kingdom in their time. When we study the saints' supernatural ministry, we see a clear historical continuity from the early Church to the modern Church.

A SCHOOL OF MINISTRY FROM THE SAINTS

I have actively researched this topic, reading any book I could get my hands on that provided reliable information on the supernatural ministry of saints through the ages. The writings, accounts, and testimonies of the supernatural ministry of many saints gave me significant insight into the authentic exercise of the power and gifts of the Holy Spirit. To some degree, I felt like I was being mentored by the saints!

Through this process, I moved beyond understanding what these saints did to discover some very practical insights about their ministries:

- how they prayed for healing
- how they received prophetic revelation and exercised prophetic ministry
- how they took bold risks in ministering to others
- intentional strategies to demonstrate the kingdom through signs and wonders
- how they understood topics that cause theological confusion in our time
- various processes they incorporated in ministry that enabled them to bear more fruit

Through this study, I felt that I had entered into a school of ministry taught by these saints! I experienced a greater understanding of the spiritual gifts in ministry, a marked increase in faith for God to use me, and an increase in my ability to partner with the Holy Spirit to demonstrate the love of God. Whether it was engaging in prophetic ministry, praying for physical healing, leading someone through inner healing and deliverance ministry, or engaging power evangelization, I saw a marked increase of fruitfulness, spiritual maturity, and greater faith to see His kingdom come and His will be done through me 'on earth as it is in heaven.' There is so much available from the saints!

I started sharing these insights at various venues and received great feedback. It was clear that the whole Church needs to have access to what these saints can teach us about ministry.

A FULL APPROACH TO THE SAINTS

For many Christians, the saints have been reduced to something like historical artifacts in our two-thousand-year history museum. The saints did amazing things that we can celebrate and receive encouragement. We acknowledge that they are with Jesus in heaven, and we call on them in faith to intercede on our behalf. But the saints are not artifacts, and they are much more than intercessors.

The truth is that God the Father has called us "to be conformed to the image of his Son" (Romans 8:29). Jesus is the model of the normal Christian life. The saints are brothers and sisters in faith who have gone before us in this process of being transformed into the image of Jesus. As Pope Benedict XVI teaches us, "the Saints are friends and models of life for us."[3] When we see them living John 14:12—doing the works of Jesus and greater works—we let them be models of how we too can live a more Christ-like life.

The Church invites us to see the saints as witnesses from whom we can learn as we seek to demonstrate the love of God to the world around us. Let us not be content to simply celebrate the miracles done through them. God is inviting us to learn from their witness, so we too can come to greater fruitfulness and maturity in Christ.

THE METHOD

Although there are many saints who engaged in supernatural ministry; I have chosen six saints for this book who exhibit particular wisdom and ministry lessons for us. Each chapter will focus on one of these saints and will include three elements:

1. CONTEXT AND OVERVIEW

I will begin each chapter by providing the context of the saint's life, including the time and place in which they lived and ministered. I will then provide a summary of the impact they made in advancing the kingdom of God in their time.

2. PERSONAL ENCOUNTER

None of these saints woke up one day and decided to start pursuing a life of miracles. Each of them experienced a transformative encounter with God that launched them into supernatural ministry. This section will detail those encounters.

3. MINISTRY LESSONS

I will then share with you the various lessons I learned from the saint's life and ministry with the Holy Spirit. These lessons provide practical and theological insights, not just into what the saints did but into how and why they did it. I believe these specific lessons can renew our minds and impart wisdom, allowing the Holy Spirit to act in and through us as he acted in and through the saints.

FAITH TO RECEIVE

In studying the action of the Holy Spirit in both the Scriptures and the lives of the saints, we see an important spiritual principle at work. It is contained in Romans 11:29: "For the gifts and the call of God are irrevocable." There is a very real connection between the gifts that God gives us and the call that he has on our life. Each of the saints you are about to learn from had a specific call . God poured out the spiritual gifts they needed to fulfill that call.

As you read this book, keep in mind the words of Revelation 19:10: "Witness to Jesus is the spirit of prophecy." I suggest that the witness to Jesus is simply hearing what Jesus has done through someone, and the spirit of prophecy is what Jesus wants to do in the future. When we read accounts of saints, there can be grace available— grace for Jesus to do the same things in the future through us!

As you enter this school of ministry from the saints, I invite you to read with expectation and a sensitivity to the Holy Spirit. If you sense a connection between the call of God on a saint's life and His calling on your life, I invite you to pray. Pray that God would pour out not simply the same anointing on you; pray rather as did the prophet Elisha, for "a double portion" (see 2 Kings 2:9)!

Now I invite you to join me in discovering, receiving from, and going on mission with some supernatural saints.

CHAPTER TWO

ST. VINCENT FERRER

CONTEXT AND OVERVIEW

As I reflect on the cultural surroundings that we find ourselves in today, I believe that the era in which St. Vincent Ferrer lived and ministered resembles our own in some significant ways. First of all, he lived during the period directly following the bubonic plague, also known as the Black Death. This was the fourteenth-century pandemic that altered normal life and led many people to live in constant fear of death.

Secondly, Vincent lived through the Western schism.

This was perhaps the lowest point in the Church's history. For decades there were two men who claimed to be the valid pope, dividing the Church in two. Not only did this conflict force everyone in the Church to take sides, but it led to outright wars in various places. Confidence in the papacy was almost extinguished.

In our twenty-first century, many of us might think that things have never been this bad. Here is a passage from St. Vincent's commentary on the moral state of Europe in his time:

> No, I do not believe that there ever existed in the world so much pomp and vanity, so much impurity, as at the present day; to find in the world's history an epoch so criminal, we must go back to the days of Noah and the universal deluge. The inns in the cities and villages are filled with persons of abandoned character; they are so numerous that the entire world is infected by them. . . . Avarice and usury increase under the disguised name of contracts. Simony reigns among the clergy, envy among the religious. . . . In a word, vice is held in such great honour that those who prefer the service of God to that of the world are held up to scorn as useless and unworthy members of society.[4]

If fourteenth-century Europe can be saved from this level of moral decay, there is great hope for us! God called Vincent Ferrer to play a particularly powerful role in reviving the Church. Today He calls us to this task, and St. Vincent can help guide us.

St. Vincent captured my attention in large part due to the extensive documentation about his life and miracles, from both historians and the official documents of his canonization. St. Antoninus attested to twenty-eight people being raised from the dead over the course of

St. Vincent's life, and 892 miracles were officially confirmed and recorded in his canonization records. Beyond the official record, historians estimate that roughly 86,000 miracles occurred through his ministry across Europe.

Through his missions, Vincent would gather crowds in the thousands, sometimes tens of thousands, in public squares across Europe. As a result of his preaching and miracles, multitudes repented. This included many kings and queens, some of whom consecrated their cities to Jesus.

Born on January 23, 1350, in Valencia, Spain, St. Vincent Ferrer received a holy upbringing in a devout Catholic family. He discerned a calling to the priesthood at an early age, and joined St. Dominic's Order of Preachers as a young adult. Through nothing less than a life-saving mystical encounter with Jesus later in his life, God called Vincent to preach repentance with apostolic boldness to a morally corrupt Church. St. Vincent would travel extensively throughout Europe, preaching the Gospel, leading multitudes to repentance, and demonstrating countless signs, wonders, and miracles to confirm the message.

A true Dominican, Vincent received advanced degrees following his ordination, including a doctoral degree. He published several philosophical and theological treatises that were very influential during his time. Vincent went on to spend most of his life serving at high-level university and even royal court positions. By the age of forty-nine, he was appointed master of the papal palace in Avignon, France.

THE *ENCOUNTER*
HEALED TO BRING HEALING

It was not long after Vincent arrived at the papal palace in Avignon that he was stricken with a life-threatening illness. He experienced intense physical pain throughout his body and lay close to death. From that pain, he prayed to Jesus in a state of full surrender. He prayed for divine healing, promising to go anywhere to preach the Gospel.

In the midst of his prayer, Vincent fell into a deep sleep. In a prophetic dream, Vincent saw himself in his room, which was suddenly flooded with a heavenly light. Jesus appeared to him, surrounded by a multitude of angels. Also present were St. Francis of Assisi and St. Dominic, who knelt together at the feet of Jesus and begged Him to heal Vincent. Jesus reached out and touched Vincent on the cheek, as if to caress his face. At that moment, two things happened.

First, Vincent recounted, at Jesus' touch he was completely healed of his sickness. Second, Jesus spoke to him "in words which the soul alone heard"[5] about his mission of proclamation and demonstration to come.

What did Jesus tell him about this mission? Three things. First, Vincent would travel to the nations preaching as an apostle. Second, his preaching would rest upon both the authority of Sacred Scripture and the confirmation of miracles. Third, his preaching would give people a merciful opportunity for repentance and conversion before Jesus' coming judgment.[6]

Following this encounter, Vincent petitioned Pope Benedict XIII to relieve him of his duties at the papal palace. Benedict XIII issued a letter that gave Vincent the highest level of authority and clearance in the Church, to preach wherever he felt called. This order would supersede the discretion of a local bishop. Thus, Benedict XIII opened the entire Church to the ministry of St. Vincent.

MINISTRY LESSONS

1 THE LANGUAGE OF THE HOLY SPIRIT

One ministry lesson for us comes from Vincent's encounter with Jesus. In his letter to Benedict XIII describing this mystical experience, St. Vincent was very clear that Jesus did not speak to him in audible words but "in words which the soul alone heard." This is a very important insight.

Often accounts of saints who heard God speak to them did not qualify the manner in which they received such revelation. On reading their accounts, we can often assume that they heard God in some kind of disruptive, clouds-parting manner, perhaps hearing his audible voice. St. Vincent understood that God speaks to us through his Spirit and in our spirit. Just as we have our five senses to take in data from the world around us, we also have spiritual faculties, and God often speaks to us through our interior faculties.

The Church has always taught this. Some great teaching on the interior spiritual senses comes from St. Thomas Aquinas. In his masterpiece, the *Summa Theologica*, he writes of the interior senses[7] and how they enable us to receive revelation, which is divine communication.

At the Encounter School of Ministry, the first part of our quarter on "Hearing God's Voice and the Prophetic Gifts of the Spirit" seeks to understand our spiritual faculties and create space to hear and discern God's interior voice. As St. Vincent and other saints testify, gaining greater familiarity with the ways God speaks opens us to the supernatural. We need to be open to these ways, not discounting inspirations but discerning the movements of the Holy Spirit that we might receive.

2 AN ANTIDOTE TO A BORING TESTIMONY

Later, in St. Vincent's letter to Benedict XIII recounting this calling, he speculated as to why Jesus would want him to confirm his preaching of repentance with miracles, signs, and wonders. He reasoned that the miracles were necessary on account of the fact that he had a very weak and boring testimony.[8]

St. Vincent grew up in a solid Christian home, received faith in Jesus at a young age, and did not go off course as a believer. Thus he did not have a sensational conversion, like those of St. Paul and St. Augustine. Indeed, Vincent considered his faith story very boring. Therefore it made sense that he would need supernatural demonstrations to convince his listeners to heed his preaching.

If you have ever considered your testimony of faith to be lacking flair, you are not alone! Follow St. Vincent's example, and pray that miracles accompany your ministry.

3 AGE DOES NOT MATTER

One other amazing aspect of Vincent's ministry is how late in life his call came. Historians believe that the average lifespan of a fourteenth-century man was forty-five years.[9] St. Vincent's encounter and call came when he was forty-nine years old. His contemporaries would have considered him very old, past his prime, and likely close to death! But throughout the next twenty years of his life, St. Vincent would traverse Europe preaching the Gospel, demonstrating the Gospel with supernatural signs, and leading entire cities to repentance and saving faith in Jesus Christ.

Many people are tempted to believe that they are too old to be used powerfully by God. St. Vincent's testimony is proof that God does not discriminate based upon age. Could God have used someone younger? Yes. But in His wisdom, He chose someone who, although advanced in years, was totally surrendered to God. Further, it can be argued that unless Vincent spent the majority of his life in the university and high ecclesial positions, he would not have had the position and favor in the hierarchy of the Church to do what God called him to do.

Recall that, prior to St. Vincent's encounter and calling in the dream, he surrendered everything to Jesus and promised to preach anywhere. A key to being used powerfully by God is the posture of surrender.

If you have ever thought that you are too old to be used by God, it's time to reject that lie. Embrace the truth: our mission is not over until Jesus says to us, "Well done, good and faithful servant" (Matthew 25:23). As long as you surrender to whatever God wants, you can expect Him to use you powerfully.

IF YOU HAVE EVER THOUGHT THAT YOU ARE TOO OLD TO BE USED BY GOD, IT'S TIME TO REJECT THAT LIE.

In my experience of Catholic culture, there is little knowledge of the supernatural ministry of St. Vincent Ferrer. Not only that, there is also little attention paid to how he ministered in the power of the Holy Spirit. For the next ministry lessons, I want to focus on some particular strategies that he employed to bring world-changing revival to a divided Church and decadent European culture.

4 STRATEGY #1: INTERCESSION

The first strategy that led to Vincent's great success was his intentional intercession. Traveling from city to city, St. Vincent spent time connecting with the heart of Jesus for each place.

Scripture says that when Jesus "saw the crowds, he had compassion on them, because they were harassed and helpless, like sheep without a shepherd" (Matthew 9:36). The Greek verb translated "had compassion" is *splagchnizomai*. The literal translation is "to be moved to one's bowels,"[10] and it is used to describe the result of witnessing injustice.

An example of this is what we experience on seeing pictures of children shriveled and starving in undeveloped nations. Something inside of us is moved, perhaps making us feel sick in our stomach and often compelling us to take action. This is the kind of response that Jesus had when he saw the crowds of people who were experiencing sickness and demonic oppression.

This is profound. Jesus did not just feel sorry for the crowds. He was physically moved because of their condition. It was from this deep compassion that Jesus ministered to the crowds.

It is with this *splagchnizomai* that St. Vincent ministered to multitudes. He postured himself in that kind of compassion. According to the Dominican historian Fr. Andrew Pradel:

"Before entering into any city, [Vincent] cast himself

on his knees, then raising his eyes toward Heaven and shedding abundant tears, he prayed for the people to whom he was about to preach."[11]

Vincent did not just say a prayer and make a spiritual offering for the city. He prayed and waited until he experienced God's compassion for the city and its people. The record indicates that his compassion was felt and expressed with tears. After receiving that compassion and praying with it, Vincent would enter the city and directly seek the principal church of the city. There he would consecrate his ministry in the city to Jesus in the Eucharist.

Yes, Jesus is present in his creation. Yes, Jesus is present in each of us as temples of the Holy Spirit. Yet as Catholics, we recognize that Jesus is fully present, in a unique and incarnational way, in the Eucharist. St. Vincent was devoted to the Eucharist and chose to begin each mission with Jesus in the Eucharist, at the center of the church of the city.

> "JESUS, I WANT TO FEEL WHAT YOU FEEL FOR THESE PEOPLE! MOVE MY HEART WITH THE COMPASSION THAT YOU HAVE FOR THEM!"

I am convinced that the power we want to see flow through our ministry starts in prayer and in experiencing God's heart for the people to whom we are about to minister. Like St. Vincent, we need to get on our knees and pray, "Jesus, I want to feel what you feel for these people! Move my heart with the compassion that you have for them!"

St. Vincent would pray until he experienced this. His lesson has given me a new standard and commitment to every mission in which I participate. I have seen a marked difference in my ministry when I commit time to prayer and then wait to receive Jesus' *splagchnizomai* for those to whom I will minister.

Although it is possible to minister out of the gifting that God has given us, there is something different and powerful when we spend time praying beforehand that we might feel what Jesus feels and think the way He thinks for those we are seeking to draw to Him in our evangelization and ministry efforts. During these times of intense intercession, I have experienced a profound shifting in my heart and then often receive many promptings and personal revelations that have led to incredible supernatural demonstrations. This is what St. Vincent did and what we can do as well.

5 STRATEGY #2: PREACHING FROM THE HEART OF THE FATHER

The second element of Vincent's success was his manner of preaching. If you remember Vincent's healing encounter, Jesus called him to preach repentance. How do you think he did that?

I would assume that a medieval friar would use "fire and brimstone" tactics to scare people into repentance. Such an assumption could not be further from the truth about St. Vincent's approach to preaching. In his *Treatise on the Spiritual Life*," he recounts his process for how to preach and lead people to repentance:

> In sermons and talks, use simple language and a homely conversational style to explain each particular point. As far as you can, give plenty of examples; then, whoever has committed that particular sin will have his conscience pricked, as though you were preaching to him alone. But it must be done in such a way that your

words do not appear to come from a soul full of pride or scorn. Speak rather out of the depths of love and fatherly care, like a father suffering for his sinful children, as if they were gravely ill, or trapped in a deep pit, whom he is trying to draw out and set free, and look after like a mother.[12]

Vincent's preaching of repentance was from the heart of a father because He knew the heart of God the Father. In his preaching, his desire was to meet the person right where they were and make them feel understood, loved, and valued. St. Vincent did not identify those to whom he preached according to their sin. He regarded them according to their potential and glory in Christ. His listeners did not receive condemnation and shame but the hope of new life in Christ.

From my study of St. Vincent, I believe that the only reason he was able to preach from the heart of the Father was that he spent so much time in prayer, specifically seeking and receiving the Father's love and compassion before ministering. The exposition of his process and mindset further reveals a high degree of sensitivity to the need of each listener. He knew that in preaching repentance, how you preach is just as important as what you preach:

> You must be like one who delights in their progress, and in the glory in heaven that they are hoping for. Such a style usually has a good effect on a congregation. For, to speak of virtues and vices in general terms evokes little response from listeners. . . . In your desire to be of use to the souls of your neighbours, you must first of all have recourse to God with your whole heart, and simply make this request of him. Ask him in his goodness to pour into you that love in which is the sum of all

virtues, through which you may be able to achieve what you desire.[13]

St. Vincent makes it very clear that simply preaching about virtue and vice, informing people of right and wrong, is insufficient. The preacher needs to be filled with the love of God! This love in your heart will overflow to those who hear you. When a soul is filled with God's love, he or she can fruitfully deliver even the harshest of corrections and explain difficult topics--including the reality of sin, judgment, and hell. Without the love of God, what we preach can be easily rejected.

Effective ministry requires much more than goodwill and good intention. It requires first receiving the outpouring of God's love and then preaching from that outpouring. For St. Vincent, this was not difficult. He was convinced that God wanted to pour out this love in those ministering, that all they needed to do was ask.

Given the opportunity to preach to groups, we first need to press into the immensity of the Father's love, as did St. Vincent.

6 STRATEGY #3: SUPERNATURAL DEMONSTRATION

Although St. Vincent was one of the most gifted preachers of his time, he was never content with good preaching. The third element of his ministry was supernatural demonstration. Right now in the Church, many ministries are engaged in intercession and preaching, but few are sold out and committed to seeing supernatural demonstration. How did St. Vincent incorporate the supernatural into his missions?

The first two strategies involved intercession, followed by preaching from the compassionate heart of

God. After his preaching, St. Vincent entered into demonstration. Historian Fr. Andrew Pradel wrote about this:

> After the sermon, he remained some time at the foot of the pulpit to bless the sick who were brought to him in large numbers and whom he often miraculously cured. A bell summoned the people at that moment and was called the Bell of Miracles.[14]

Replica of St. Vincent's Miracle Bell at St. Vincent Ferrer Church in New York City. Photo Credit: Lauren Gentry.

Now we see a fuller picture, and it is amazing! After Fr. Vincent's preaching from the Father's heart, his team would bring out a bell and ring it. They named it "the miracle bell." This bell signaled the sick to come forward and receive prayer for healing.

And multitudes were healed! From the available testimonies, it appears that most of the healing miracles that flowed through Vincent's ministry happened in this context of intentional time for healing prayer, following the proclamation of the Gospel in Vincent's preaching.

Now, it may appear that there was a very structured split in how Vincent ministered: that he would simply preach the Gospel, pause to shift into healing prayer, and start ministering in the power of the Spirit. This is not the case. St. Vincent's missions did not follow a predetermined schedule; the Spirit led him. His preaching was marked by frequent words of knowledge for healing as well as mystical encounters that were impossible to predict:

> He paused at times himself to weep, and to calm his emotions; at other times it was to foretell some event or to work a miracle. In a word, these interruptions were often caused by his ecstasies, and when the rapture had ceased, he would take up the thread of his discourse as if nothing had occurred.[15]

Let me provide an example of what this looked like. One day, while preaching in Lleida, Spain, to an immense multitude, including the king of the region, Vincent received a word of knowledge. Right in the middle of his discourse, he said that a paralytic man was a couple miles away, struggling to reach the city. Upon hearing this declaration, the king dispatched two of his servants in the direction Vincent indicated. They found the paralytic just as Vincent had described and brought him back to the city.

Carrying the paralytic in their arms, the servants approached St. Vincent, who raised his hand and made the Sign of the Cross over the cripple. The man was instantly healed, and he ran to St. Vincent to thank him. After the crowd witnessed this healing, Vincent went on with his preaching.

This story makes me wonder what was going through St. Vincent's mind when he received the prompting to call out about the crippled person. How do you know that a particular image or prompting you receive is actually revelation from God or just a product of your imagination? The only way to find out is to respond to the prompting and take a risk! As you step out and take risks for God, you come to learn which promptings are from Him and which are not.

St. Vincent appears to have cultivated mature discernment of the prophetic revelations he received. That maturity led to incredible demonstrations like this one, which helped lead an entire city to repentance.

> AS YOU STEP OUT AND TAKE RISKS FOR GOD, YOU COME TO LEARN WHICH PROMPTINGS ARE FROM HIM AND WHICH ARE NOT.

I started taking intentional risks in the area of words of knowledge when I was a youth minister, in my twenties. I would pray prior to youth nights and ask God to reveal to me words of knowledge for the students he wanted to bless. In the most pastoral way possible, I would share what I received with the various students and discover whether or not the knowledge and accompanying words were pertinent to their lives.

Over time, I became aware of promptings that were true versus those that were just off. Whether they were words of knowledge for healing or words about something going on in someone's life, those that were on point were different from those that were not. Let me give you two examples.

Before one of the youth ministry nights, I asked Jesus for words of knowledge about any students He wanted to bless. I received one impression about a student's home situation. When I approached the student and shared with him what I had sensed in my prayer, he told me that was not accurate at all. It was kind of embarrassing.

But in spite of the error, he was really excited that I was praying for him. He invited me to pray with him about another situation and overall the effort was not a failure.

Later I took note of the mode and manner in which I had received the word about the student's home life. I concluded that it was not one of the trusted ways God speaks to me.

Not long after this experience, during my prayer before the youth ministry night, I received knowledge that one of the teens–let's call her Jennifer, a senior in high school–was invited to a birthday party by a guy she liked. The manner in which I received this felt much different than the previous experience. I also sensed that she was the only girl invited and that it was not a healthy situation. I finally got the sense that if all of this was true, then Jesus did not want her to go to the party. During the small group portion of the youth night, I approached Jennifer, explained what I received for her during my prayer before the youth night, and asked if any of that was true.

She looked completely shocked. All of it was true. The problem is that she already accepted the invitation and felt too much pressure to back out of the party happening in 3 days. I prayed for her to have the courage to make the right decision. The next week she came back and reported that she ended up backing out of the party and felt amazing about the decision. I realized that my risk could have potentially saved her from a very harmful and life-altering mistake. These experiences helped me discern which word was coming from God and which was coming from me.

Taking small risks helped build my faith, to the point that now I have greater confidence to go after and minister in words of knowledge, even at large events and missions.

At the Encounter School of Ministry, during our quarter on "Hearing God's Voice and the Prophetic Gifts of the Holy Spirit," we create an environment in which students can practice receiving and sharing words of knowledge for one another. Students receive immediate feedback and are able to grow in discernment, maturity, and faith.

7 IMPARTATION

In studying and receiving from the life and ministry of St. Vincent Ferrer, I was perplexed with a serious logistical question: with the tens of thousands of miracles that happened throughout his twenty-year ministry, was St. Vincent the one person praying for healing during his missions? The answer is no. And in pursuing this question, I found what could be a significant breakthrough in our understanding of impartation.

"Impartation" is a term used to describe the transference of a spiritual gift or grace operating in the life of one person to become operative in the life of another person. The term comes from Paul's words to the Romans, "For I long to see you, that I may *impart* to you some spiritual gift to strengthen you" (Rom 1:11, RSVCE, italics added). This transference of graces through the ministry of others can be clearly observed throughout Scripture, such as in the lives of Moses (see Numbers 11:25), the prophet Elijah (2 Kings 2:9-15), and St. Paul (Acts 19:6). St. Vincent would pray for an impartation of his spiritual gifts to those partnering with him.

I believe this dynamic is still at work in ministries today. At the Encounter School of Ministry and at most of our conferences, we invest time in teaching on this reality before praying for impartation. We go to great lengths to build an atmosphere of faith to receive prayer for impartation and we have received an incredible amount of testimonies that demonstrate the reality and fruitfulness of impartation.

Impartation is not in any way comparable to the grace offered to us in the sacraments of the Church. Rather it is part of the mysterious charismatic workings of the Spirit, who gives graces to the Church through her members.

The idea of impartation has been viewed with skepticism and concern by some people in the Church, including some leaders. Since this term and the corresponding experience are not familiar in the experience of most Catholics, it can lead some to assume that prayer for impartation is a modern aberration that should be avoided. Yet prayer for impartation is apparent in Scripture, and we can also see St. Vincent's incorporation of it to great effect in his ministry.

Historians of St. Vincent attest that on multiple occasions, he was unable to pray for all the people who needed a miracle. His response to the demand for his prayer ministry was to impart the gifts of his life to others, so that they could pray for the needed miracles. Vincent is quoted as saying on more than one occasion: "I have wrought sufficient miracles today and I am tired. Do yourself what is asked of me; the Lord who works through me, will also work through you."[16]

> HIS RESPONSE TO THE DEMAND FOR HIS PRAYER MINISTRY WAS TO IMPART THE GIFTS OF HIS LIFE TO OTHERS, SO THAT THEY COULD PRAY FOR THE NEEDED MIRACLES.

Although St. Vincent acknowledged his effectiveness in ministry, he had confidence that such could happen through any faithful disciple of Jesus. He had faith that God could use anyone. So he routinely prayed that the power and gifts he had received would be imparted to others.

An example of this occurred when a priest from Lleida invited St. Vincent to visit a generous benefactress of his order who was grievously ill. St. Vincent's response is priceless:

> You ask me to go and see this person that I may heal her by a miracle; why do you not do it yourself? Go, I give you my power, not only for this infirm person, but also for all whom you may meet on the way.[17]

The priest then went to see the crippled benefactress. On his way, he came across five individuals who were suffering from various wounds. Following Vincent's instruction, he stopped to minister and pray for each one. To his surprise, everyone he prayed for experienced immediate physical healing.

The priest continued to the home of the benefactress. There he prayed for her, and later he recounted that she was immediately restored to perfect health. This gifting remained with the priest for the rest of his life.

Could God have given this priest the gift of healing directly? Absolutely! But in God's wisdom and good pleasure, he often chooses to involve us in his plan, even in the distribution of spiritual gifts.

It is important to note that, given the clear historical record of St. Vincent engaging in the impartation of his spiritual gifts, we can presume that he did so with wisdom and understanding about the action of the Holy Spirit. Just because a person prays for a particular spiritual gift or grace to be shared does not mean that it happens automatically. Impartation does not take place the way the sacraments do, *ex opere operato*, "by the work worked."[18] Rather the transference happens in the realm of faith, mystery, and ultimately the will of God.

We should not be surprised when we receive a spiritual gift of grace through another's prayer for impartation. God loves to share His spiritual gifts with us, and He loves to respond when we ask to share with others the gifts that we have received. The apostle Paul exhorts us to "earnestly desire the spiritual gifts" (1 Corinthians 14:1, RSVCE). The only reason we can "earnestly desire" spiritual gifts is that we have a Father who earnestly desires to give them.

As we receive gifts from our Father, we should be on the lookout for His promptings to pray and share the gifts we have with others, so they can be strengthened in their mission and ministry.

8 MEETING SUSPICION WITH HUMILITY

One of the unfortunate realities of stepping out in faith to demonstrate the love of God through the power of the Holy Spirit is that other Christians do not always receive our ministry well. The pursuit of supernatural ministry can often be met with suspicion.

In the ministry of Jesus, signs and wonders were continuously met with suspicion by religious leaders. If Jesus experienced this, we should not be surprised if we experience levels of opposition when we step out in faith to see signs and wonders released in Jesus' name. St. Vincent experienced this.

Although we do not have all the details, there is an account of St. Vincent's ministry being met with suspicion from his superiors in the Dominican order. Even though he had the full support of Pope Benedict XIII, Vincent was under obedience to his religious order, the Dominicans. His superior was troubled by all the miraculous claims surrounding Vincent's ministry, and he decided that he needed to investigate. In the meantime, he forbade Vincent to pray for miracles.[19]

From a human perspective, St. Vincent would have every reason to resist and possibly even reject such an unjust response from his superior, given the incredible fruit already borne in his ministry. But we are not called to reason from a human perspective. In Matthew 16, after Peter objected to Jesus' prophecy that he would die in Jerusalem, Jesus corrected the apostle: "Get behind me, Satan! You are an obstacle to me. You are thinking not as God does, but as human beings do" (Matthew 16:23).

Peter's problem was thinking from a human perspective. St. Vincent approached the matter from a heavenly perspective. He humbly submitted, committing himself to not perform any miracles until his superior reviewed his ministry.

Soon after this suspension, St. Vincent was walking through town. A pair of stonemasons were repairing a building a few stories in the air, and one of them turned to greet Vincent from his scaffolding several stories up. The workman lost his balance and began falling headfirst to certain death. St. Vincent commanded him to stop falling and the man did. He was left suspended in mid-air. This caused quite a stir in the town.

Vincent told the suspended stonemason that he needed to leave but would return shortly. He ran to the Dominican oratory and brought his superior outside. He showed his superior the stonemason and asked for permission to complete the miracle. His superior was shocked and immediately gave him permission. Vincent commanded the stonemason to be lowered to the ground.

This miracle was visible to the whole town. In fact, what Vincent did was so prominent that to this day there are multiple paintings depicting the miracle. Needless to say, after this encounter, Vincent was released back into full ministry, and the suspicion ended.

What is the best part of this account? St. Vincent did not have to exonerate himself. God vindicated him and brought justice. He did so supernaturally. All Vincent had to do was choose humility and obedience. This is the exact response we need to have when our ministry is held in scorn or suspicion by a Church authority. What could this look like in our time?

Let me give you an example.

When my good friend Dan DeMatte and I were producing Encounter Radio for EWTN out of the Columbus, Ohio, affiliate station, St. Gabriel Radio, we both were filled with an incredible confidence that God would touch our listeners in a supernatural way. We started praying for and releasing words of knowledge at the end of our shows. Some of the words were related to physical conditions that we believed the Lord wanted to heal. As we received and discerned such words, we would call out the physical condition and any details about what we believed God wanted to heal.

The shows were pre-recorded, and they aired up to two weeks later. We started receiving testimonies through our website of people healed.

After a few weeks of ending our shows with words of knowledge, one of the station managers came in and expressed concern about this practice. We were gently asked to hold off and let the station chiefs consult with members of the board for direction. Even though we had received multiple testimonies from listeners, we submitted.[20]

Within the week, we received a voicemail from a woman who was listening in her car to one of our last shows. She had been in a car accident a few years prior, in which she experienced a torn rotator cuff. Even with a full year of physical therapy, she was not able to raise her arm over her head.

At the end of the show, the woman heard us call out a word of knowledge that God wanted to heal a woman with a torn rotator cuff that never healed properly. I instructed the listener to raise their arm over their head. This woman did so while driving her car, and she felt the Holy Spirit come upon her. She was healed in an instant! She experienced Psalm 107:20: "He sent forth his word, and healed them" (RSVCE). The woman pulled over to praise God, with tears of rejoicing!

What makes this story even better is that this woman happened to be the wife of one of the St. Gabriel Radio board members. The board member contacted the station managers to report the miracle. The next week, we were free to release as many words of knowledge as we felt called by God to share!

> WHEN WE CHOOSE HUMILITY IN THE FACE OF OPPOSITION, IF GOD IS WITH US, THEN ALL WE NEED TO DO IS WAIT FOR HIM TO MOVE ON OUR BEHALF.

Jesus promised that "Whoever exalts himself will be humbled; but whoever humbles himself will be exalted" (Matthew 23:12). When we choose humility in the face of opposition, if God is with us, then all we need to do is wait for him to move on our behalf.

9 OVERCOMING ERRORS REGARDING DISCOURAGEMENT AND MEDICINE

"These signs will accompany those who believe...They will lay hands on the sick, and they will recover" (Mark 16:18, 19). Our involvement in Jesus' ministry of healing is His idea.

At the Encounter School of Ministry, we have an entire quarter on power and healing. In this quarter, we partner with the Holy Spirit to equip our students to participate more fully in the healing ministry of Jesus in the world around them. Throughout the years of equipping and pastoring students in healing ministry, many have been tempted to fall into either of two errors about healing.

On the one hand, many students who have been involved in praying and seeing Jesus supernaturally heal have experienced various degrees of sickness and infirmity in their own lives. In the absence of healing from their conditions, some have expressed doubt about God's ability to continue to use them to bring healing to others. They tend to disqualify themselves from praying for another person's healing.

Anyone who has ever struggled with this should be encouraged to know that St. Vincent actually dealt with some serious health issues along his journey and throughout his ministry. Toward the end of his life, he developed infirmities that prevented him from walking long distances and standing with full strength. Did these circumstances stop him from preaching the Gospel, praying for and seeing physical healing in others? No!

St. Vincent knew that healing was not about him. It was about Jesus working through him, regardless of his current health! St. Vincent focused so completely on what God was doing and calling him to do that he did not allow the circumstances of poor health to stop his mission. Many people experienced healing miracles through his ministry even in the midst of his poor health.

> ST. VINCENT KNEW THAT HEALING WAS NOT ABOUT HIM. IT WAS ABOUT JESUS WORKING THROUGH HIM, REGARDLESS OF HIS CURRENT HEALTH.

If you are dealing with health issues, that does not disqualify you from being used by God to bring His supernatural healing! At the same time, do not stop persevering in seeking full healing for yourself. One of my favorite testimonies on this point comes from my friend Dr. Mary Healy. As a trusted curriculum advisor and instructor at the Encounter School, Dr. Healy shared a testimony during one of her sessions about this topic. She went to visit a close friend named Tim and his wife Michelle, who were both members of the first graduating class of the Encounter School. Tim was also in the midst of suffering from stage four cancer. Leading up to her visit, Mary had been dealing with significant pain in her hips that eventually got worse causing her to limp. During her visit, the couple offered to pray for her healing. After the prayer, they checked in with her and she didn't feel any pain. In the next few days, the pain did not come back and Mary realized that God healed her through the simple prayer for healing from a man with advanced cancer and his wife! The good news is that you don't have to be healed to see healing flow through your prayer.

This leads us to the second error. Some students have been tempted to believe that because Jesus can respond to their faith and supernaturally heal them, they should not pursue natural means of healing through doctors and medicine. They fear that pursuing natural means could be an offense against faith and thus prevent them from receiving divine healing.

Anyone who has struggled with this thought should be assured to know that, even though thousands of healings flowed through his ministry, St. Vincent received the best natural health care of his time. He received surgery at one point, and historians note that he endured the resulting pain without complaining. He also is known to have taken medicinal herbs, which were noted as being repulsive to ingest.

St. Vincent's example is an excellent application of the exhortation given to us in the Book of Sirach:

> Make friends with the doctor, for he is essential to you;
> God has also established him in his profession.
> From God the doctor has wisdom,
> and from the king he receives sustenance.
> Knowledge makes the doctor distinguished,
> and gives access to those in authority.
> God makes the earth yield healing herbs
> which the prudent should not neglect. (Sirach 38:1-4)

Errors are often the exaltation of one extreme against another--in this case, prayer for healing against natural medicine. When we acknowledge that both are from God, then we can position ourselves to receive the healing that God wants to give us in whatever form He makes available.

St. Vincent Ferrer, pray for us!

CHAPTER THREE

ST. PHILIP NERI

CONTEXT AND OVERVIEW

St. Philip Neri is known as both the patron saint of joy and the apostle of Rome.

In the sixteenth century, Rome had fallen into moral decay and the Church into a rigid clericalism where many men sought the priesthood as an avenue for worldly advancement. Priests often neglected their sacred duties and sought temporal pleasures and power. Through the life and ministry of St. Philip Neri, a genuine and gradual revival of faith took place. This revival fueled the next generation of saints and missionaries and furthered renewal in the Church.

Although Philip is well known for starting a congregation and the communities of prayer and mission called oratories, Church historians say that he converted the city of Rome one person at a time. Isn't this a beautiful contrast with St. Vincent Ferrer? While God called St. Vincent to minister to crowds, God called St. Philip Neri to minister to one person at a time.

Philip was born on July 21, 1515, in Florence, Italy. Like St Vincent, he was raised in a very devout Christian home. He loved to learn, and he pursued studies in philosophy and theology. Throughout his youth he was captivated by the city of Rome. As a young adult, he sold everything of value and moved to the Eternal City, where he would be ordained a priest at the age of thirty-five.

Philip went on to form what he called the oratory, a community of men seeking holiness, community, and mission. In 1575 his oratory received the official papal seal of approval, and today it is known as the Congregation of the Oratory of St. Philip Neri. Oratories would spread all over the world; they were instrumental in the life and ministry of St. John Henry Newman hundreds of years later, and they continue to impact the Church today.

By the end of Philip's life, the worldly pursuits of the clergy and moral decay in Rome had greatly diminished. The people of Rome saw St. Philip become the personal confessor to the last three popes of his life. They also witnessed how he manifested the gifts of the Holy Spirit in his ministry and evangelization.

There is much faith and wisdom to receive from studying the life and ministry of St. Philip Neri. Documents from his canonization process, along with biographies from his disciples— particularly Fr. Antonio Gallonio and Fr. Giacomo Bacci—offer countless testimonies of Philip' supernatural ministry, including individuals being raised from the dead.

THE *ENCOUNTER*
RECEIVING PENTECOST FIRE

After his arrival in Rome as a young adult, Philip decided to make frequent pilgrimages to the seven major churches there. He cultivated Jesus' heart for the lost and developed a daily devotion to the Holy Spirit. During this season, Philip committed himself to daily prayer for more of the Holy Spirit and the spiritual gifts. When he was twenty-nine years old, Philip experienced a life-changing encounter with the Holy Spirit.

On the vigil of Pentecost in 1544, Philip was led to go to the catacombs of St. Sebastian in Rome to pray. While he was in prayer, the Holy Spirit showed up much as he did at the first Pentecost. Philip saw a ball of holy fire descend. This fire entered his mouth and lodged in his heart. There followed several powerful manifestations of the Holy Spirit:

- Philip began to shake with violent tremors.
- He fell to the ground and experienced the intense fire of God's love.
- He experienced a tangible heat from this fire and a profound joy that would mark his life from then on.
- Two of his ribs broke, and his heart grew to twice the normal size. This fact would be confirmed in a postmortem autopsy.

The outpouring of the Holy Spirit was so intense that

Philip cried out, "Enough, Lord, enough! I cannot take any more." [21]

I absolutely love this account. The manifestations that Philip experienced are very similar to those that are increasingly present when we gather to pray for more of the Holy Spirit and His gifts at our conferences and ministry events.

Some Catholics are skeptical of these kinds of sensational manifestations. Many have only heard of these things happening in a Pentecostal, Protestant context. But while the Pentecostal movement did not begin until the early twentieth century, we can look at the amazing ministry of the early Church and identify the upper room events as the reason for the disciples' fruitfulness.

> WHEN WE PRAY FOR MORE OF THE HOLY SPIRIT AND HIS GIFTS, WITH A SINGLE AND DEDICATED FOCUS, WE SHOULD NOT BE SURPRISED WHEN HE SHOWS UP AND WE EXPERIENCE SOME PROFOUND MANIFESTATIONS.

In a similar way, we can connect the grace on St. Philip's life and ministry to the outpouring of the Holy Spirit he experienced in 1544. When we pray for more of the Holy Spirit and his gifts, with a single and dedicated focus, we should not be surprised when He shows up and we experience some profound manifestations.

MINISTRY LESSONS

1 THE ACTION OF THE HOLY SPIRIT IN MINISTRY

After reading the many eyewitness accounts of Philip ministering to the people of Rome, I started to see a very interesting common element in these reports. Basically, the way in which the Holy Spirit came upon Philip at his Pentecost encounter often showed up again when he prayed for others. I want to propose a ministry principle to you: The way that the Holy Spirit has come upon you is often a sign of how he will come through you.

THE WAY THAT THE HOLY SPIRIT HAS COME UPON YOU IS OFTEN A SIGN OF HOW HE WILL COME THROUGH YOU.

There are numerous testimonies of these manifestations during St. Philip's prayer with others. Bacci's biography offers fourteen references to St. Philip shaking or trembling when he ministered and prayed over people. Allow me to share just a few of these testimonies.

The first comes from St. Philip's ministry to Cardinal Girolamo Panfilio, who fell sick and was judged by doctors to be close to death.

> Philip went to visit him twice a day; and once, when the malady was at its worst, moved by the spirit of God, he took the sufferer by the head, and held it tightly with

both his hands. Meanwhile he trembled and was agitated in his usual way, while he prayed for him, and when he had finished his prayer, he said, "Be of good cheer, and do not be afraid; you will not die this time, but in a few days you will be free from your complaint." Panfilio began to mend immediately, and in a short time was completely well. [22]

St. Philip was aware of Jesus' promise that believers would lay hands on the sick and they would recover (see Mark 16:17-18). This is how he ministered.

Bacci notes that when Philip laid hands on the cardinal, a physical trembling and agitation accompanied his prayer. He further notes that such occurrences were normal in Philip's ministry. Philip then received a prophetic word about the efficacy of the prayer and declared to Panfilio that he would recover. The best part of the story is that the healing began immediately, and the recovery was complete soon after.

Another testimony in which we can see the manifestation of the Holy Spirit involves a woman named Lucretia Cotta, who was afflicted with heart and eye problems. Philip was her regular confessor. When learning of her health conditions, he invited her to come to the chapel to receive prayer for healing. According to Lucretia:

> He told me to kneel down. Then St. Philip Neri put one hand [over] my heart and one hand on my eyes and prayed. I felt that his hand was shaking as well as his whole body. . . . [S]ince that day I had no heart problems. [23]

Again, Philip's prayer for Lucretia was accompanied by shaking under the power of the Holy Spirit. Lucretia's testimony continues:

Some days later when I went to confession with St. Philip Neri, our saint put his hands on my eyes, praying and shaking a lot. I was left as blind. St. Philip Neri told me not to fear; that it would not remain that way. After praying an hour [for me] I began to see very well and my eyes returned to their place and to this day I continue [to be healthy] and I always have this as a miracle of St. Philip Neri.[24]

So the first day Philip prayed, there was healing of the heart. The next time he prayed specifically over Lucretia's eyes. In her sixteenth-century testimony, she again notes that his hand was shaking. Another interesting fact is that during this prayer, Lucretia's eye condition got worse. This reality appears to have encouraged Philip and strengthened his resolve. He pressed on for an hour, till there was a sustaining breakthrough.

Another account describes perhaps one of Philip's biggest risk-taking moments. Pope Clement VIII was bedridden and experiencing intense pain. Although many people were interceding for the pope, it is one thing to pray for a person's healing from afar and another thing to go and minister directly. Philip felt prompted to go and pray over the pope. This is what happened:

When [Philip] came into the room, his Holiness, who from the acute pain could not bear any one to touch even the bed he lay on, told him not to come any nearer. Philip, however, continued to advance until he was close by the side of the Pope, who again bade him stop and not on any account to touch him. Philip then said, "Your holiness need have no fear," and forthwith he caught hold of the Pope's hand, and with much affection and zeal, and with his wonted trembling, he pressed it, and the pain ceased; so that the Pope said,

"Now you may continue to touch me, for I feel great relief."[25]

In reading of these manifestations of the Spirit, it is clear that the trembling and various manifestations served as trusted signs to Philip of the action of the Holy Spirit upon him for ministry. I would not be surprised if the trembling and shaking increased his faith and helped fuel the boldness that would be needed to disregard the pope's direction and bring a healing breakthrough!

As you will see in several of the testimonies, manifestations of the Spirit often accompanied St. Philip's prayer over people. Why? Because the way that the Holy Spirit has come upon you is often a sign of how he will come through you. After the Holy Spirit pours himself out upon us, we should not be surprised if, in ministering to others, we experience the signs that were present when his life poured into us.

2 RESTING IN THE SPIRIT

As the Holy Spirit is renewing the Church with his power and gifts, many people are experiencing what appear to be new actions of the Holy Spirit. One of these experiences has come to be known as "resting in the Spirit." The term refers to being overwhelmed by the Spirit to the point that the person can no longer stand up and even appears to be unconscious. Often people who experience this are overwhelmed by the presence of God and experience a deep personal encounter with Jesus. At healing services, it is common for people to be receiving prayer and suddenly collapse onto the floor because of the action of the Holy Spirit present through the prayer for healing. These people might then rise up and realize that they are healed from their condition.

Some leaders in the Church have been critical of this experience and have shared their concerns with us. Most often the skepticism is rooted in their assumption that these experiences have not happened in the history of the Church or the lives of the saints and are therefore some kind of aberration from pure Catholic Christianity. Is this true?

It is here that we can receive our next ministry lesson from St. Philip, involving a man named Prospero Crivelli. This man was literally on his deathbed; the doctors said there was no hope. Prospero told those attending him that he was assigning all his property to Philip Neri. News of this made its way to Philip, who wanted nothing to do with his friend's wealth.

Philip hastily made his way to Prospero's sickbed, and according to the account of Gallonio who was present: "[Philip] then prayed, with tears running down his face, and laid his hands on the dying man, who immediately fell into a sound sleep, astonishing as it is to relate."[26]

Let's stop right here. This is a sixteenth-century, direct account of Philip Neri laying hands on a sick man and praying over him. The man lost consciousness. Did he fall into a natural sleep, or was this supernatural? How long did this sleep last?

The testimony goes on: "The dying man woke from his sleep, having slept for about 15 minutes, and discovered that his health returned, to the astonishment of the doctors."[27]

Those present did not have any terminology for this action of the Holy Spirit. Today we would conclude that Prospero experienced something supernatural—far beyond a fifteen-minute nap—that resulted in divine heaing. The presence of the Holy Spirit for healing was released upon him through the prayer and ministry of St.

Philip that was so overpowering that he appeared to be asleep.

This testimony is very important to us in our time. Resting in the Spirit is not just a twenty-first-century phenomenon of the charismatic renewal. It is an action of the Holy Spirit that was happening five hundred years before the charismatic renewal existed!

3 FAITH TO RELEASE THE MANIFEST PRESENCE OF GOD'S LOVE

In His final prayer to the Father before the crucifixion, Jesus declared, "Now this is eternal life, that they should know you, the only true God, and the one whom you sent, Jesus Christ" (John 17:3).

The Greek word that we translate "know" is *ginoskō*. This word refers to an experiential or felt knowledge as opposed to cognitive or intellectual knowledge. The type of knowledge that Jesus wants us to have is personally felt and experienced.

St. Philip lived and ministered during a time when, although almost everyone was raised in the Christian faith and received intellectual knowledge of God, most people had no personal experience of the love of God in Christ Jesus. It was in the absence of that encounter that the Christians in Rome fell into the level of spiritual decay that plagued the city. Is this context much different from ours today?

Philip believed that everyone needed to experience a personal touch from God and encounter His love for themselves. He would often meet people who were distressed about their relationship with God and clearly did

not know the love of God at the experiential level. He had

so much confidence in God's desire to make His love known to people that he would simply offer to pray for them to encounter God's love for themselves. What did this confidence look like?

> Once there was someone in distress, needing to experience God's love, and Philip responded, "I will pray for you, and you shall feel it," and in fact the person felt himself moved with such an extraordinary fervour, that he came all trembling to acknowledge it as a gift of the Saint.[28]

What incredible faith! There was no doubt in Philip's mind that Jesus would manifest His love. This person had an encounter with God's love, described as "extraordinary fervour," accompanied by "trembling."

Further, Philip did not pray for them to encounter God's love at some point in the future. He prayed with the confidence that the encounter could happen right then, on the spot.

God wants to pour out and bring others to encounter his transforming love. He needs us to boldly pray. When we pray in faith, God moves. We get to witness Him break into people's lives and see His kingdom advance in them.

A man named Giovanni Aturia shared a testimony of receiving prayer from Philip Neri to encounter God's love. After the prayer, "I felt many good desires kindled in my mind, in a way which made me think that a particular grace was descending upon me from heaven."[29]

What a beautiful visualization of our prayer ministry. When we pray, heaven comes to earth and descends upon those for whom we are praying.

GOD WANTS TO POUR
OUT AND BRING
OTHERS TO
ENCOUNTER HIS
TRANSFORMING
LOVE. HE NEEDS US
TO BOLDLY PRAY.

There are many such testimonies of Philip praying with people who then had profound experiences of God's love. In response to these experiences, St. Philip said, "This is milk which our Lord gives to those who begin to serve him."[30] Philip understood that in order to begin the journey of discipleship and real holiness, people need to personally feel God's love. He understood that such consolation is as normal for a new follower as milk is for an infant.

Prior to my work at Encounter Ministries, I served as a youth minister for nine years in different parishes. Like St. Philip, I cultivated great faith for Jesus to manifest His love to those who had never known it. Many students I ministered to were raised in good Catholic homes, received good instruction and formation, but had never encountered Jesus personally. I came to see that unless these young people had an encounter, they were more likely to fall away from their practice of the faith after high school. I made it a priority to create opportunities to pray for these students to experience the love of Jesus.

On one large regional retreat with multiple youth groups, after preaching about the depth of Jesus' love for us in the Holy Spirit, I offered to pray for any student one-on-one. A high school girl came up and told me that she had never experienced God's love and that she had been wounded by the people closest to her. She started to share all the reasons why she was too far from God's love to experience Him in her life. I stopped her and asked if I could just pray for her. She agreed.

St. Philip was very affectionate when he prayed with people; he would often hold the person's face in his hands or fully embrace them. In the most appropriate manner possible, I gently embraced this girl and simply prayed, "Jesus, please show her how much you love her right now. Jesus, please show her how much you love her right now."

"JESUS, PLEASE SHOW HER HOW MUCH YOU LOVE HER RIGHT NOW."

I waited. After a few moments, the girl moved from anxiety and distress to weeping. She described how the love of God flooded over her. I simply held her, thanked Jesus, and prayed that He continue. This encounter went on for several minutes. I knew that something life changing was happening. The girl thanked me and went back to her friends.

A few years later, I ran into this young woman again, at an Encounter Conference. She told me how that moment of feeling Jesus' love through my simple prayer transformed her life and set her on the path of full discipleship with Jesus. She expressed her gratitude for my ministry, and we praised God for his breakthrough.

The manifestation of God's love is supernatural, beyond anything we can give. As did St. Philip, let us pray for God's love to flood those who have never encountered it. And let us cultivate the faith that when we pray for people who need to feel God's love, they will!

4 UNDERSTANDING HEALING MINISTRY

When you read the many accounts of Jesus ministering to individuals who came to him for healing, you might find it interesting that Jesus did not release healing in the same way all the time. There were different modes and manners in which he brought the healing. Consider the following:

- For the woman who was crippled and unable to stand up straight for eighteen years, healing came with the *laying on of hands* (see Luke 13:13).
- For the man born blind, Jesus performed a *prophetic act* of smearing spittle over his eyes and instructing him to wash it off (John 9:6).
- For Peter's mother-in-law, Jesus *rebuked the fever*, and it left (Luke 4:39).

You might ask, "What caused Jesus to minister healing differently in these different circumstances?" That is the wrong question. The proper question is not "What" but "Who caused Jesus to minister healing differently in different circumstances?"

Jesus proclaimed, "the Son can do nothing on his own, but only what he sees the Father doing" (John 5:19). He also said, "I do nothing on my own, but I speak these things as the Father instructed me" (John 8:28, NRSVCE). In his ministry on earth, Jesus remained completely dependent on and obedient to His Father, to the point that he admittedly only did and said what his Father showed him. This is the key to understanding why Jesus ministered healing in different ways. It was what His Father was revealing in each circumstance.

Since Jesus did everything he saw his Father doing, we can rightfully conclude that the Father was leading him to minister healing in different modes. In a similar way that Jesus was dependent on the leading of the Father in His ministry, we are dependent upon Jesus in our ministry. Jesus taught us, "Those who abide in me and I in them bear much fruit, because *apart from me you can do nothing*" (John 15:5, NRSVCE, italics added).

Just as Jesus was completely dependent on the Father, we are completely dependent on the guidance of Jesus in our ministry. The practical elements of healing ministry involve asking Jesus how He wants us to pray and then praying according to the particular way in which He inspires and directs us. St. Philip understood this reality. We see in the countless healing stories that he ministered healing in different modes, as Jesus directed him.

> JUST AS JESUS WAS COMPLETELY DEPENDENT ON THE FATHER, WE ARE COMPLETELY DEPENDENT ON THE GUIDANCE OF JESUS IN OUR MINISTRY.

5 ANOINTING OF THE SICK

In reading through the two eyewitness biographies of Gallonio and Bacci, I found astounding the number of healings that happened in a direct, one-on-one manner. Before reading these accounts, I assumed that St. Philip brought healing through the Sacrament of the Anointing of the Sick. In case you are unaware, this sacrament involves anointing the sick person with sacred oil and praying the established liturgical prayers over them. This sacrament is seen two places in Scripture. First, in Mark 6:13, the disciples "anointed with oil many who were sick and cured them." Then the Letter of James gives the following counsel:

> Is anyone among you sick? He should summon the presbyters of the church, and they should pray over him and anoint [him] with oil in the name of the Lord, and the prayer of faith will save the sick person, and the

65

Lord will raise him up. If he has committed any sins, he will be forgiven. (James 5:14-15)

The apostle James makes it clear that not only is this anointing one of the modes by which God can heal but that it is the presbyters, the ordained leaders in the local Church, who administer this sacrament. In Catholic teaching, only ordained clergy are permitted to administer the Sacrament of the Anointing of the Sick.

What I learned in my study of St. Philip is that none of his healings came through the Sacrament of the Anointing of the Sick. In fact, Gallonio and Bacci shared seven healing testimonies that came through Philip's ministry after the person received the Anointing of the Sick but did not improve.[31]

This is helpful to know, because we have encountered a significant number of Catholics who believe that, because the Anointing of the Sick is a sacrament, it is more efficacious than other modes of ministry. Often these people are only open to receiving their desired healing through the sacrament. Although we can have faith in God to heal in a particular way, we ultimately have no control.

Consider the story of the crippled man at the pool of Bethesda (see John 5:1-9). An angel of the Lord would stir up the waters of the pool, and the first person to get in the water would be healed. The man believed his healing would come through the angelic intervention, but it ended up coming through Jesus' word of command - "Rise, take up your mat, and walk" (John 5:8).

This fact should not diminish our faith in healing through the Anointing of the Sick. St. Philip himself was physically healed through the sacrament. In 1577 Philip recovered from a serious, life-threatening illness, but nine years later,

Philip was struck down by a sudden recurrence of his sickness, in a virulent and dangerous form. However he recovered from it rapidly, after being anointed with holy oil, despite expectations, and to the surprise of the doctors who called it a miracle.[32]

Do not discount the healing power of this sacrament!

Now, back to Philip's ministry. Of all the healings that occurred as a result of his prayer ministry, most were accomplished through either the laying on of hands or the prayer of command. I will discuss the laying of hands first and then the prayer of command.

6 LAYING HANDS ON THE SICK

We have already referred to Jesus' promise that those who believe "will lay hands on the sick and they will recover" (Mark 16:19). St. Philip had great faith in this promise. On numerous occasions he was prompted to simply lay his hands on a person and pray. The resultant healings were in fact so numerous that Bacci wrote an entire chapter titled "Of the miracles wrought by the touch of Philip's hand."[33]

For example, in 1566 a man named Pietro Vittrici was bedridden because of a serious disease. The doctors had given up on him, and his family had started to mourn his death. "Philip then came to him, laid his hands on the dying man, and prayed for him; the result was that he immediately began to feel much better, and two days later was able to get out of bed quite well."[34]

When a person of great faith in the healing love of Jesus comes through the door of someone with very little or no hope of recovery, based on the natural signs of an illness, the sick person's chances of recovery get a lot higher. This was the way Philip lived.

In another account, a man named Maurizio Ancrio was in a poor state of health, with internal pain and many alarming symptoms. The doctors were convinced that he was dying, since he had lost his speech and his pulse was barely detectable. Philip went to pray for him:

> Then he placed his hands on the sick man's head and stomach, and immediately afterwards went away without saying a word. At the moment of Philip's touch the sick man perfectly recovered his health; his speech was restored, and his pulse became strong and even; all the pain ceased, and not a trace of weakness was left behind.[35]

Would Philip lay hands and pray only once? No. He would often lay hands, pray, check on the person, and see improvement or continue to pray if needed. This is very important.

For example, a woman named Giulia Lippi suffered from severe headaches that would last for days at a time. The headaches would come out of nowhere and leave her almost disabled. When she was at one of St. Philip's Masses, one of these splitting headaches came on, and she could not even get home. She came to Philip.

> "Father, I have not strength to go home, for my head is well nigh bursting with pain." Then Philip, trembling as usual, began to pray, and took her head between his hands, pressing them gently together, and then said to her, "Well, how do you feel now?" "Better, Father," she said, "but not well." Then Philip again pressed her head, and asked a second time how she felt; and this time she answered, "I am quite well."[36]

After his first prayer, he checked in and re-interviewed Giulia. She indicated improvement but not complete healing. Although a partial and incomplete healing might discourage some, it only encouraged St. Philip and he pressed in and persevered praying again. It was in the next prayer that she indicated her restoration. Praying for healing was not St. Philip's idea. Healing is Jesus' idea. Philip participated in this ministry to great effect and always under the promptings and inspiration of the Holy Spirit. Many times he was inspired to simply lay hands on the sick and pray in faith.

This mode of prayer, however, is not the only way we can be inspired to pray for healing.

7 THE PRAYER OF COMMAND

One of the modes of prayer that Jesus used was the prayer of command, which we see in the healing of Peter's mother-in-law. A prayer of command is a spoken, authoritative act of faith addressed to the body, a sickness, pain, or an evil spirit. In the case of Peter's mother-in-law, Jesus spoke to the condition (the fever), and it left her (see Matthew 8:14-15). At other times, Jesus commanded a person to function in the way God had designed them, even though their condition prevented that. The command released healing in the body, enabling the person to do what Jesus said. An example of this is the healing of the paralytic in Mark 2:1-12. Jesus commanded the man to rise, pick up his mat, and go home. This command released the healing, allowing the man to obey.

The theological basis for our participation in the prayer of command is the authority Jesus gave his disciples in Matthew 10:1, "authority over unclean spirits to drive them out and to cure every disease and every

> A PRAYER OF COMMAND IS A SPOKEN, AUTHORITATIVE ACT OF FAITH ADDRESSED TO THE BODY, A SICKNESS, PAIN, OR AN EVIL SPIRIT.

illness." Examples of the prayer of command would be "In the name of Jesus, I command the bones, ligaments, muscles, and tendons to be healed" and "Rise and walk in Jesus' name."

We teach our students that the prayer of command should be prayed according to the leading and prompting of the Holy Spirit. When the Holy Spirit inspires a disciple to pray a prayer of command, we see some amazing healings. It should be noted that the prayer of command is not directed at God, commanding Him to heal. The idea of commanding God is insane. Rather, the prayer of command is directed at the sickness or infirmity present in the body.

Essentially the prayer of command is an expressed act of faith. We exercise our authority in Christ over the sickness and infirmity as the Holy Spirit leads us. At the Encounter School, in our quarter "Power and Healing" we create an atmosphere of faith for students to learn and start praying for healing over one another. We accompany them as they grow in discernment and maturity.

Just as there has been confusion over manifestations of the Holy Spirit, there has also been confusion regarding the prayer of command in healing ministry. Our Encounter School curriculum has undergone a thorough theological review by a team of Catholic theology professors, to ensure that it is free from moral and doctrinal error and rooted deeply in Scripture, official Church teaching, and the testimony of the early Church Fathers. This includes our teaching on the use of command prayers.

Unfortunately, we have still experienced some significant opposition to the use of command prayers in healing ministry. Many find it problematic because it does not seem to be evident in the lives of the saints and the history of the Church. Fortunately for us, St. Philip gives ample evidence of the use of command prayers in non-sacramental healing ministry.

In fact, Bacci titled an entire chapter of his early biography "Of Philip's miracles, which he worked by commanding the disease to depart."[37] This chapter includes the testimony of Maria Felice de Castro in Torre di Specchi, who experienced an intense fever and was wasting away over a hundred successive days. Maria Felice believed that she was nearing death. She called for Philip Neri and asked him to pray for her healing. This is what happened:

> Then the Saint put his hand on her head, and holding it there for a while, spoke these words, "I command thee, fever, to depart, and leave this creature of Almighty God," and from that day forth the fever was [gone], and Maria was completely restored.[38]

Philip spoke to the condition with the authority he had in Jesus over sickness and infirmity, and the sickness left. Philip was able to minister in this way because he knew his identity in Christ and his corresponding authority.

Did St. Philip believe that he could say a prayer of command and heal every person who came to him? According to the accounts of his ministry, especially what we can see in the next lesson, the answer is no. Philip understood that praying with authority always comes from being "in Christ." The Holy Spirit makes Christ present to us. The only way Philip would pray a prayer of command and see healing was if Jesus inspired him to pray that way.

Philip provides valuable insight into incorporating the prayer of command for healing in ministry. We can take great comfort in knowing that such command prayers, following the guidance of the Holy Spirit, are deeply rooted in our Catholic tradition.

8 TENSIONS IN HEALING MINISTRY

As the body of Christ is becoming more active in healing ministry, at Encounter Ministries we see a tension arising among people engaged in it. On the one hand, we know that every individual who came to Jesus for physical healing was restored to health. This fact demonstrates Jesus' desire to heal and should increase our confidence and expectation for Jesus to heal through us. On the other hand, we know from experience that not everyone we pray for gets healed.

> THE REALITY IS THAT ALL SUPERNATURAL HEALING IS ULTIMATELY TEMPORARY: EVEN LAZARUS, WHOM JESUS RAISED FROM THE DEAD, HAD TO DIE AGAIN.

Some have made the argument that we do not see more healing because we are not fully convinced that God wants to heal every person in every circumstance. Should we expect God to physically heal every person, every time we pray?

At Encounter we believe that although Jesus does want to heal much more than we realize as a Church, it would be presumptuous and ultimately a great error to hold that every person should be healed through every prayer. The reality is that all supernatural healing is ultimately temporary: even Lazarus, whom Jesus raised from the dead, had to die again. Death is the ultimate reality for each one of us, a reality that a healing ministry must take into account. God has not only a plan for our life but also a plan for our death. The ultimate goal of healing ministry is to be a sign that confirms the Gospel message.

St. Philip understood this reality and navigated this tension with the Holy Spirit. Although there are countless healings recorded through his ministry and Philip had great faith in Jesus' desire to heal, he was never presumptuous in his prayer.

Philip was invited by a woman named Marcello Vitelleschi to pray for her husband, Virgilio, who was sick and close to death.

> Philip told Marcello Vitelleschi that when he really wished to pray for [Virgilio's] recovery, he found himself deprived of the power to pray, and he seemed to hear an interior voice telling him that it was necessary for Virgilio's good that he should die then.[39]

Philip shifted his ministry to ensuring that Virgilio's soul was healthy. The man died soon after their time together.

This is a marvelous example of how we should likewise address the tension: always pray with expectant faith for a person's recovery, unless we become convicted by the Holy Spirit that God is calling the soul to Himself. In that case, we should do all we can to ensure that the person is in right relationship with God.

Should we vocalize our discernment with the sick person? Absolutely not. That would be a great offense against charity. Could we be wrong in our sense that God is preparing them for death? Absolutely! But even if we are wrong, we can do no harm by ministering to the health of their soul.

Because we might be wrong in our discernment, we should continue to pray for healing. But in the midst of our prayer, we can subtly address the need of ensuring good spiritual health. For example, "Is there anyone you need to forgive?" "Is there anything you need forgiveness for from God right now?" "Can we ask Jesus now?"

Like St. Philip, we need to remember that physical healing is not the destination. It is rather a sign that points to the final destination: a healed and restored relationship with God for eternity.

9 THE CONTINUED ACTION OF THE HOLY SPIRIT IN PERSONAL PRAYER

With so many stories involving manifestations when Philip prayed for people, it is important to know that these things happened even outside ministry situations. In describing Philip's prayer life, his disciple Fr. Antonio Gallonio tells us that many times,

> He was so pierced by God's love that he was forced to lie down on his bed as if he were ill and weak. He would turn his face to heaven, singing psalms with both spirit and mind. When he kindled a fire of meditation, as we have already heard, he would tremble all over, and become heated with the force of the heavenly flame.[40]

In the same way that the Holy Spirit first came upon Philip, He continued to come upon him in personal prayer! We should not be surprised when the Holy Spirit continues to renew and refill us!

10 LIGHTHEARTED JOY

You may be tempted to think that because Philip had profound and very serious encounters with God, he must have been a very serious person. This was not the case at all. As I already mentioned, Philip is considered the patron saint of joy. His joy was like a magnet that attracted countless people to him and through him to Christ. Philip's joy actually looked like something. His joy was full of laughter and light-hearted humor. Let me share a few stories.

At one point a prominent cardinal was coming to Rome, and this man had a reputation for being a little too worldly. The cardinal fawned over his pet dog. Philip decided to pull a prank. He would do the cardinal "a favor" by taking his dog on a walk—without letting the cardinal know.

Philip then made his followers carry the dog around the streets of Rome on a silk pillow, making a great spectacle of the dog and most likely causing much laughter. The dog ended up loving Philip and his followers more than the cardinal. In fact, he did not return to the cardinal.[41]

In another account, Philip was walking down one of the streets of Rome, and he saw Ignatius of Loyola walking with a few other leaders of the Jesuit order. The Jesuits appeared very solemn, proceeding with great resolve and serious expressions on their faces. Philip thought that the pace of Ignatius's life was a little too serious at that moment, and perhaps these men needed a little joy. Philip nodded to his companions and secretly ran up behind Ignatius, knocked his biretta off his head, messed up his hair, and ran away laughing. Initially upset, Ignatius quickly realized the joyful prank and laughed off the antics of Philip. He proceeded with a smile on his face.

Stories of the joyful pranks of St. Philip are encouraging because they provide a good snapshot of genuine joy that is fully human. They remind us not to take ourselves too seriously and to live life to the full in the service of the Gospel.

Philip and Ignatius were contemporaries, both operating in Rome. While Philip was bringing the Gospel to Rome, Ignatius and the Jesuit missionaries were bringing the Gospel to the ends of the earth. Ignatius would eventually claim that no one led more men to join the Jesuits than Philip Neri. Ignatius and Philip were canonized on the same day, March 12, 1622, along with St. Teresa of Avila and St. Francis Xavier.

St. Philip Neri, pray for us!

CHAPTER FOUR

ST. CATHERINE
OF SIENA

While I was doing my initial research for this project, I called Dr. Mary Healy, the Encounter School curriculum advisor, and shared with her the progress I was making, including some exciting lessons from St. Vincent and St. Philip. I then asked if she could recommend female saints who ministered in the power and gifts of the Holy Spirit and whose story could provide trusted insight. She answered without hesitation, "You have to cover St Catherine of Siena!"

I was initially confused. All I knew about St. Catherine was that she had some very profound mystical encounters with Jesus, was recognized as a Doctor of the Church, and told the pope to move the papacy back to Rome from Avignon. Now, after some study of her life, I have to say that no other saint has provided more wisdom for ministering in the power of the Holy Spirit.

CONTEXT AND OVERVIEW

The person we know as St. Catherine of Siena was born to Lapa Piagenti and Giacamo Benincasa on March 25, 1347. She came from a very large family in Siena; she was the twenty-third of twenty-five children! Her father was a cloth dyer, and their family home was located next to his business.

"Caterina," as she was known, personally encountered Jesus when she was a young child, and she immediately committed her life to Him. From a young age, she cultivated a deep prayer life, desiring solitude and contemplative union with Jesus.

Caterina never felt called to religious life, but she did join the third order of lay Dominicans at a young age, and she experienced a spousal union with Jesus. Her entire life would be guided by profound encounters with Jesus, which initially transformed her and eventually led to her being a major leader in the Church and someone of influence in the secular world. She became a trusted counselor and confidant to bishops, cardinals, and popes as well as an ambassador for kings and queens of the Italian city states.

What was more profound than Catherine's leadership influence was the supernatural ministry that she demonstrated throughout her life. She manifested all the spiritual gifts, with a particular anointing for deliverance ministry and prophetic ministry. There is much we can receive from Caterina!

THE *ENCOUNTER*
A CALL TO CONTRADICT

Catherine had a very unusual childhood. From her early encounter with Jesus at the age of six, she cultivated an almost completely contemplative life. This drove her mother crazy and created a lot of tension in their home. This tension ceased when the Lord revealed to her father, Giacamo, that everything Catherine was experiencing was really from Him. Giacamo then declared his full support for Catherine's life of dedicated prayer and gave her a small room in the home. There she would eat her meals, alone with Jesus in prayer.

When Catherine was around the age of twenty-one, she experienced another life-changing encounter—this time with Jesus' wounds. It would shift her into a new lifestyle of evangelization and ministry.

Catherine was in her room alone, and Jesus spoke to her: "Go seat yourself at table with your family. Talk to them kindly and come back here." Catherine broke into tears, for she was not prepared to leave her life of contemplation. Jesus responded that he was preparing to shift her life and use her as his instrument of evangelization:

> Today I have chosen unschooled women, fearful and weak . . . but trained by Me in the knowledge of the divine, so that they may put vanity and pride to shame. If men will humbly receive the teachings I send them through [women] I will show them great mercy, but if they despise these women they shall fall into even worse confusion and even greater agony.[42]

Jesus is the original feminist and pursued the authentic empowerment of women. This kind of call would have been completely shocking in the fourteenth century. Can you imagine how Catherine would have responded? She responded just as Mary the Mother of God did to the Angel Gabriel, with a simple yes. She rose and joined her family for supper. Seeing their introverted daughter join their world came as a shock to her parents.

> JESUS IS THE ORIGINAL FEMINIST AND PURSUED THE AUTHENTIC EMPOWERMENT OF WOMEN.

This simple act of faith in the calling of Jesus on her life initiated Catherine's life of active ministry. One biographer notes that "her familiarity with the secrets of the supernatural world became more apparent to the world around her."[43]

Catherine's writings offer many ministry lessons for us. So does the testimony of her closest disciple, Blessed Fr. Raymond of Capua, OP, who would eventually become master general of the Dominican order.

MINISTRY LESSONS

1 ENTERING INTO DELIVERANCE MINISTRY

Jesus promised that if we believe in Him, we will do what He did and even greater things (see John 14:12).

One thing He did a lot was cast evil spirits out of oppressed people. About this He declared, "If it is by the finger of God that I drive out demons, then the kingdom of God has come upon you" (Luke 11:20).

Delivering people from the influence of evil spirits is a direct sign of the kingdom of God breaking into this world. Jesus wanted everyone to know that the kingdom of God looks like something and that it can be clearly identified by witnessing people set free from the torment of evil spirits. We need to appropriate this truth. And of all the works and ministries of Jesus, the one Catherine arguably became most famous for was deliverance ministry.

This ministry began with a need. The Monaldo family of Siena had a daughter named Lorenza who experienced what appeared to be demonic attacks. She developed debilitating cramps in her body. The family found out that on occasion their young daughter was able to speak fluent Latin, without any training. The local religious sisters responsible for educating their daughter discerned an evil spirit afflicting the child.

Her parents first took Lorenza to the relic of a saint who was known to free people from demonic influence. This did not work for their daughter. They then brought her to the Church, and she received the rite of exorcism. This did not set her free either.[44]

The parents then decided to take her to Catherine and ask her to pray for her. Catherine's response was:

"I am myself tortured every day by evil spirits (likely referring to temptations), I do not need to take up the fight against other people's demons."[45]

The Monaldos would not take no for an answer. They sought out Catherine's spiritual director,

Fr. Tomasso, who told her to help them. Catherine agreed, instructing the family to drop their daughter off at her home. The girl came to her room, and Catherine stayed up all night in spiritual battle with the demon.

In the morning, there appeared to be a great deal of progress and perhaps complete freedom. But Catherine discerned that the girl was not completely free. She decided to have the child stay in the house another day.

Later in the day, Catherine made the mistake of entrusting Lorenza to other people so she could run an errand. In her absence, the girl was left alone. Catherine returned to find Lorenza raving, cramping up, and causing great disturbances.

> As soon as the virgin saw her she said, "Ah, you infernal Dragon! How dare you invade this innocent little maiden again? But I have full confidence in the Lord and Saviour Jesus Christ, my Heavenly Bridegroom, that this time you will be driven right out and never come back again!" With these words she took the girl with her to the place where she prayed.[46]

Catherine engaged in full and persevering confrontational deliverance throughout the night. She later told Raymond of Capua what happened. He wrote of the deliverance:

> I questioned the holy virgin about it secretly, myself, especially because it looked as though that particular devil had been given license to refuse to give in either to the relics or to exorcism. She told me that that evil spirit had been so obstinate that she had had to fight him all through the night until four o'clock in the morning, she commanding him in the name of the Saviour to

be off, and he refusing with unprecedented stubbornness. After a long struggle, realizing that he would be forced to leave Lorenza, he said, "If I come out of here I will enter into you." Immediately the virgin had replied, "If the Lord wills it so, and I know that without His permission you can do nothing, God forbid that I should prevent you, or in any other way alienate myself from His will or set myself up against Him." Whereupon the proud spirit, struck amidships by such humility, lost nearly all the power he had over the little girl; but he still hurled himself against her, attacking her throat and causing changes and swellings there. Then the virgin placed her hand on the little girl's neck, made the sign of the cross, and so freed her from that affliction too.[47]

In this first deliverance, Catherine persevered in prayer and stood firmly on the authority of Jesus over the evil spirit. And Catherine remained completely safe from any attack.

It is important to know that there is a formal difference between simple deliverance prayers made in faith and the rite of exorcism. Catherine was not engaging in a solemn exorcism; rather she was ministering from her faith in Jesus using simple deliverance prayers of command.[48] As noted by Blessed Raymond, the rite of exorcism had been previously employed and had not brought Lorenza freedom.

Lorenza returned to her family, and she never showed any more signs of demonization. In fact, this deliverance that Catherine ministered to her was a pivotal point in her spiritual life. Lorenza eventually followed God's call to religious life and entered the convent.

2 PROTECTION FROM DEMONIC ATTACK

Before I go into the next lesson, I must share with you some background information. One of the most common questions we receive regarding deliverance ministry is whether or not lay people are able to cast out evil spirits. One of our Encounter School online students wrote us the following typical letter:

> Dear Encounter,
>
> My priest told me that lay people do not have the authority to cast out demons and that I should therefore not be involved in any kind of deliverance ministry. I'm very confused. Please help.

This question and others like it come in response to a widespread opinion that prayers of command are only licit if the person praying has some kind of established authority over the person to whom they are ministering. In this mindset, lay people can do deliverance ministry only for family members and perhaps a few others over whom they have some kind of authority.

A further contention is that lay people open a door to spiritual attack and demonization if they attempt to cast out an evil spirit from someone over whom they have no authority. The fear is that the evil spirit could come into the person ministering and demonize them. The conclusion often drawn is that only priests have the authority to cast out demons, and lay people need to cease engaging in this kind of ministry.

This thinking can lead to a mindset of helplessness, clericalism, and fear.

A team of trusted Catholic theologians have reviewed these claims and demonstrated that such restrictions err in the following ways:

- They are contrary to Scripture and the express words of the Lord: "These signs will accompany those who believe: in my name they will drive out demons" (Mark 16:17). Jesus did not say that these signs accompany priests and bishops but rather all who believe!

- They are contrary to Tradition (the teachings of the Church Fathers, St. Thomas Aquinas, Alphonsus Liguori, and others).

- They are not taught by the Magisterium.

- They induce an unhealthy fear of demons and a sense of helplessness.

If you are interested in reviewing the full response of this team, please check out the deliverance FAQs on our website.[49]

Now back to Catherine. If it were true that lay people do not have authority to cast out evil spirits or that they open themselves to spiritual attack in doing so, then St. Catherine of Siena could not have done what she did in her deliverance ministry. Catherine was a lay person. According to Blessed Raymond of Capua, she "commanded evil spirits, and cast them out of the bodies of the possessed."[50]

Catherine had no natural or ecclesial authority over any of the people from whom she cast out evil spirits. What she did have was an ability to use the baptismal authority Jesus gave her. Her intimacy with God gave her tremendous faith in His power over the devil. Catherine never experienced any open doors to demonization from her ministry. She is acknowledged as a Doctor of the Church, so her teaching and ministry bear significant authority.

Now, it is very important to note that the possibility of encountering spiritual attack as a result of deliverance ministry is very much a reality; in fact, to some degree, it should be expected. At the same time, we should expect protection in Christ even more. Catherine carried this kind of expectation. How did she do it?

Jesus declared to his disciples, "All authority in heaven and on earth has been given to me" (Matthew 28:18, RSVCE). If Jesus has all the authority, then the devil has none. The only authority the evil one can ever have is that which we give him. How do we give him authority? One way is to believe the lie that he has authority over us.

In Catherine's ministry to Lorenza, the demon threatened Catherine shortly before it was cast out:

> "If I come out of her, I will enter into you." Immediately the virgin had replied, "If the Lord wills it so, and I know that without His permission you can do nothing, God forbid that I should prevent you, or in any other way alienate myself from His will or set myself up against Him."[51]

The devil is a liar and the father of all lies (see John 8:44). He lied about his ability to oppress Catherine. I believe the key to her protection from this threat was her conviction of the absolute authority of Jesus. This is clear in her response. She simply declares the truth, that Jesus' will in this matter is supreme.

Jesus said, "You will know the truth, and the truth will set you free" (John 8:28). Jesus already spoke the truth about our protection in Luke 10:19: "I have given you the power 'to tread upon serpents' and scorpions and upon the full force of the enemy and nothing will harm you." When we believe the truth that the devil has no authority over us and Jesus' promise that nothing will harm us, we can be confident in our freedom, even when demons make their vile, empty threats.

> IF JESUS HAS ALL THE AUTHORITY, THEN THE DEVIL HAS NONE. THE ONLY AUTHORITY THE EVIL ONE CAN EVER HAVE IS THAT WHICH WE GIVE HIM.

3 INCREASED FAITH FOR DELIVERANCE MINISTRY

Catherine continued to step out in faith in Jesus' ministry of bringing freedom to those oppressed by demons. The stories of her deliverance ministry are so many that Blessed Raymond of Capua titled an entire chapter of his book on her life "The Devil's Enemy." One important lesson comes from seeing how Catherine matured and increased in faith for deliverance ministry.

Raymond's account of Catherine's ministry demonstrates a clear growth in her faith for deliverance. In the deliverance of Lorenza Monaldo, it took Catherine hours, some mistakes, and multiple prayer sessions before the girl was set free from her demonic oppressor. Later in her deliverance ministry we see that people were set free much faster and more easily. One testimony in particular attests to this fact.

A female servant of Catherine's friend Mona Bianchina was tormented by an evil spirit. Mona resolved to bring her servant to Catherine for deliverance prayer. When she brought her servant unannounced, along with a small group of friends, including a friar named Santi, Catherine was on her way out the door to arbitrate peace between two enemies. Instead of sending Mona and her servant away or canceling her trip to arbitrate the peace, Catherine commanded the demon to be still until she returned, and the demon obeyed. Raymond records the scene:

> Turning to the woman possessed, she said, "But so that you, Enemy, will not hinder [my mission of peace], put your head on this person's knees and wait there until I come back." At this command the woman possessed meekly laid her head on the hermit Friar Santi's knees— it was he who told me that he was the one the virgin pointed out to the woman—whereupon the virgin of the Lord went off to accomplish her mission of peace. In the meantime the Devil was howling through the mouth of the one possessed, "Why are you keeping me here? O, let me go away."[52]

The group remained in the room while Catherine was gone. The possessed woman kept still, with her head on Friar Santi's knees. The testimony continues:

> When Catherine came into the room [the demon] began to howl, "O, why are you keeping me here?" And the virgin answered him, "Get up, you miserable creature, and be off with you at once; leave this creature who belongs to the Lord Jesus Christ alone and never again dare to torment her!" Then the evil spirit, as he went out

of the woman, left as it were sobs behind in her throat, and a swelling. The virgin put her hand to her neck, made the sign of the holy cross over it, and drove away the wicked spirit; and so, in the presence of all, restored the woman to perfect health. As the poor woman was still aching and stunned from the violence of what she had gone through, the virgin held her up for a time with her arms, letting her lean against her breast; then she got the others to give her something to eat so that she could go home fully recovered. And this was done.[53]

The difference between this deliverance and the one with Lorenza is clear. The first deliverance took multiple prayer sessions and included a lot of demonic manifestations; overall it was very messy. Mona's servant was set free much faster and much more easily. Catherine had clearly matured in her deliverance ministry.

What was the reason for her growth? Sigrid Undset, one of the most thorough historians of Catherine's life, notes that although Catherine was initially reluctant to enter into deliverance ministry, "she finally overcame this fear of demons who tortured other people and indeed became famous for her power to cast out unclean spirits."[54]

Catherine went into the first deliverance with some degree of fear, and I believe that accounted for the mess and difficulties. Once she dealt with her fear, as Undset notes, her deliverance ministry bore great fruit.

The devil works through fear. To the degree that we allow fear to influence us, our ministry will be inhibited. We mature in our deliverance ministry to the degree that we overcome the influence of fear.

This principle is true across all ministries. I have realized that if I'm afraid someone's not going to get healed or my prophetic word will not impact someone the way I sense it should, the fruit is not there.

WE MATURE IN OUR DELIVERANCE MINISTRY TO THE DEGREE THAT WE OVERCOME THE INFLUENCE OF FEAR.

Throughout Scripture there are constant reminders that we need to break through fear. The Apostle John says, "There is no fear in love, but perfect love drives out fear" (1 John 4:18). Jesus is perfect love. As we allow Him to pour His love into our lives, there is less room for fear.

This is absolutely true for anyone engaged in deliverance ministry. Catherine responded to Jesus' love in confronting the demon oppressing Lorenza. She broke through the fear and walked on in great faith and maturity in her deliverance ministry.

4 RELEASING PROPHETIC VISION

Jesus declared, "My sheep hear my voice; I know them, and they follow me" (John 10:27). Jesus is the good shepherd; we are his sheep. He says that we can hear his voice. This happens through His Spirit living in us.

Personal prayer includes our experience of hearing God's voice for ourselves. Prophetic prayer includes our capacity to hear God's voice for the world around us. The Second Vatican Council teaches, "The holy people of God shares also in Christ's prophetic office."[55] Because we share in His prophetic office, we share in Christ's prophetic ministry. St. Catherine was famous not only for her deliverance ministry but also for her prophetic ministry.

At the Encounter School of Ministry, we spend an entire quarter on hearing God's voice and growing in prophetic ministry. During this quarter, students first grow in their confidence in hearing God's voice for themselves and then for the world around them. They invest time in becoming aware of the languages of the Holy Spirit and the ways that God speaks to us through our spiritual faculties. Much of the maturing process that occurs in prophetic ministry involves learning how to process and apply the various kinds of revelation we receive in our prophetic ministry.

I have learned a lot from the descriptions of how Catherine perceived and released revelation to lead others closer to Christ. Fr. Raymond of Capua said that of all the supernatural deeds that came through her ministry, there was one that was the greatest. This greatest miracle provides a valuable lesson on one aspect of prophetic ministry.

The miracle involved two men convicted of heinous crimes and sentenced to death. As part of their sentence, they were chained, put on a cart, and pulled through the town to their place of execution, being tortured on the way. During this process the men expressed no remorse or repentance for their crimes, and they refused a priest's attendance for Confession and last rites. Instead they chose to shout blasphemies against God throughout their journey to death.

As the men were taken by Catherine's house, she heard their blasphemies and immediately started praying for their conversion:

> You saved the robber who hung on the cross beside you,
> even though he was justly condemned for his crimes;
> save these two miserable men who were created in your
> image and redeemed by Your precious blood—or will
> you permit that they shall first suffer these cruel tortures
> before they die and then go to eternal agony in hell?[56]

Catherine then saw these men journeying on the cart to their death, and she saw—through the revelation of Holy Spirit—evil spirits lurking around them and encouraging them in their blasphemy. The evil spirits became aware of Catherine's presence; then she cast them out. Once they were gone, she saw an image of Jesus crowned with thorns, bleeding from his torture—as if he were suffering personally for these men.

Catherine released this vision to these men in her prayer. At that moment, the two men saw the same vision of Jesus. They were moved to sorrow for their sins at the realization that Jesus suffered for them, and their defiance broke. Raymond of Capua recounted:

> A ray of Divine Light penetrated their hearts; they
> asked repeatedly for the priests, and confessed their
> sins to him with visible signs of grief. Then they turned
> their blasphemies into songs of praise and, making a
> public declaration that they deserved the punishments
> they were undergoing, and other far worse ones, went
> towards their death happily, as though invited to a
> wedding.[57]

These men died right after experiencing full and genuine conversion, all because of Catherine's prophetic prayer ministry. This ministry involved direct revelation from God through her and then to the men. We should pause here and break down the action of the Spirit.

Catherine was moved to compassion for the men because of their blasphemy and impending trip to hell if they did not repent. Confident in her relationship with God, she made a bold prayer to Jesus for their souls. She then received the revelation of Jesus being scourged for them personally. As her biographer Sigrid Undset put it, "By concentrating the whole power and intensity of her soul on them, she could convey what she was thinking and what she saw to the two criminals."[58] In faith she released the revelation she received from Jesus through the Holy Spirit. The two men reported the same revelation of Jesus, which led to their salvation.

This is a very important lesson for our prophetic ministry. Sometimes God gives us a revelation and a corresponding interpretation that he wants us to share with someone, to lead them closer to Christ. At other times, as St. Catherine experienced here, God shares with us a revelation that we are supposed to simply share with another person - in Catherine's case, through the Holy Spirit directly. Part of the prophetic maturity process comes in growing to understand this distinction in your ministry.

What does this look like? An example comes from our good friend Fr. Brian Gross. Fr. Brian, from the Diocese of Bismarck, North Dakota, had a life-changing experience at the 2018 Encounter Conference. The following year, he did a one-semester priestly sabbatical at Encounter Ministries headquarters in Brighton, Michigan. He has since led conferences for us, to great effect.

Fr. Brian told me of a parishioner who came to his office seeking counsel regarding difficulties in his marriage. We'll call the man Joe. Joe was your average Sunday Mass Catholic who prayed before meals and loved his family. Fr. Brian tried unsuccessfully to bring some wisdom to Joe's marital situation. Then he asked Joe if they could bring it to the Lord and pray together. Joe agreed.

Fr. Brian led a simple prayer, inviting the Holy Spirit to come, and then he waited. In this process he received an image in his mind of Joe standing in a pit. In the pit were two staircases leading out of it, with two figures standing at the top. Fr. Brian discerned that this was not an image he was supposed to interpret but one he was to give directly to Joe. The conversation then looked something like this:

Fr. Brian: *I see you in a pit.*

Joe (with his eyes closed): *Uh-huh. I am right there. I see the stairs.*

Fr. Brian: *Why don't you go up the stairs?*

Joe: *OK. I'm going up the stairs. I see two people at the top. I'm getting closer. Oh, my goodness! It's Mary and Jesus! They are here for me! Jesus is so beautiful! He's so beautiful! Do you see this?*

Fr. Brian: *OK, Jesus, show Joe what you want to do next.* [Almost immediately Joe buckles over and starts crying. This goes on for a few minutes.]

Fr. Brian: *What's going on, Joe?*

Joe: *My stepdad and my brother are here as well. They are hugging me right now! My stepdad died a few years ago, and my brother died twenty years ago. I've been blaming myself for his death and have felt responsible. That weight is now gone!*

This prophetic encounter took fifteen minutes, and it revealed the root trauma that was causing the issues in Joe's marriage. Jesus addressed it and healed it because

Fr. Brian had the faith and maturity to receive the revelation for Joe and recognize that it was meant to be shared directly with him.

This was not some new and strange form of ministry. It has been happening throughout the history of the Church. As we learn from how the saints engaged in prophetic ministry, we become intentional about the ways of the Holy Spirit, and God can entrust greater revelation to us for the good of others!

5 THE EXPERIENCE OF PRAYERS OF COMMAND FOR HEALING

As I have studied the various modes by which the saints prayed for and saw supernatural healing in their ministries, the most common mode they used was the prayer of command. In the last chapter, we saw how St. Philip Neri incorporated prayers of command for healing. St. Catherine was also known for the many healings that flowed through her commands. In our experience at Encounter Ministries, most of the healings that we have seen, though not all, have come through the prayer of command.

This does not mean that the prayer of command has greater power than other modes of praying for healing--for example, the laying on of hands, prophetic acts, and prayers of petition. The power

> THE POWER COMES IN OUR OBEDIENCE TO THE PROMPTING WE RECEIVE.

comes in our obedience to the prompting we receive. What does a prompting look like? Although it is ultimately going to be different for different people, St. Catherine provides us with a very valuable lesson on being

95

prompted to pray a prayer of command for healing.

In the year 1390, there was an outbreak of the plague, killing many people in Siena. After a series of body pains, including swelling in the groin and a splitting headache, the plague would cause infection in various organs. This would lead to an intense fever, often culminating in death.

While serving the sick in Siena, the rector of the local hospital, Messer Matteo, contracted the plague. After a few days of the illness, a doctor did a test and reported that "there is blood in the liver, a common feature of this pestilence; and I am therefore afraid that the [hospital] will soon find itself without its worthy Rector."[59]

Those close to the rector began preparing for his death. Fr. Raymond was one of those present, and he recounts the following:

> In the meantime [Catherine] had heard that Matteo had been struck down by the plague. As she was very fond of him because of his virtues, she hastened to see him, fired by charity and as though angry with the plague itself, and even before she reached him she started shouting from a distance, "Get up, Messer Matteo, get up, this is no time for lying in a soft bed!" At the words of this command the fever and the swelling in the groin and all the pain immediately disappeared, and Matteo felt as well as if he had never been ill at all. Nature had obeyed God through the mouth of [Catherine], and at the sound of her voice his body had been restored to perfect health.[60]

Raymond is very clear about Catherine's response to learning that Matteo was struck by the plague: it was one of righteous anger toward the plague itself. This prompted her to issue the prayer of command.

Being prompted to pray a prayer of command can at times be less of an intellectual movement and more of a visceral reality. This experience of righteous anger against sickness and disease can indicate that God is giving us His authority in faith over the condition we are angry toward. How does this work?

Sickness and disease were not part of God's loving design of humanity. All sickness, suffering, and death have their roots in the tragedy of original sin in the Garden of Eden. From an eternal perspective, sickness and disease are like hostile oppressors whose presence is ultimately an injustice to the children of God.

It is like the anger I feel when my children are on the playground and some bullies start to harass them. What is the appropriate response? Get angry over the injustice. Take authority over the situation. Make my presence known, and command those bullies to get lost.

When we experience authentic righteous anger against sickness and disease, we are sharing in Abba Father's heart for his child who is suffering at the hands of a hostile oppressor. Like St. Catherine, we can recognize the authority we have and utilize the prayer of command for healing.

It is important to know that we cannot manufacture this experience of righteous anger. It is ultimately a gift. If we experience it and respond with authority in Christ, we should not be surprised when the body responds to our prayer of command.

6 THE INTIMACY THAT INFLUENCES HIS WILL

God's will is the ultimate determining factor of all reality. When entering into any kind of ministry, our goal should always be surrender to His will. Surrender is the ultimate posture of peace.

Christians sometimes develop the mindset that because God's will is sovereign, we play no part in what God will or will not do. This is a great error.

In Exodus 32, while Moses was receiving the Ten Commandments from God on Mount Sinai, the Israelites chose to create their own god, a golden calf, and to worship it. This not long after witnessing all God's miracles to free them from Egypt. Upon witnessing the Israelites' blasphemy, God declared to Moses that he was going to wipe out the people and start over.

How did Moses respond? He didn't say, "This is very difficult, but you are God, and I am just going to surrender it to you." No. Moses pleaded with God to relent in his wrath against their sin. How did God respond to this plea? "So the LORD changed his mind about the punishment he had threatened to inflict on his people" (Exodus 32:14). A mystery revealed here is that God's will in certain matters can be contingent on what those in relationship with Him ask for.

CATHERINE DEMONSTRATES THIS KEY TO INFLUENCING GOD'S WILL: INTIMATE FRIENDSHIP WITH HIM.

The reality is that God's will is not a cut-and-dry matter. Like Moses, we can play a role in influencing God's will. Why? We receive the answer in the next chapter, when God tells Moses, "You are my intimate friend; You have found favor with me" (Exodus 33:12). At the heart of the concept of influencing God's will is that God calls us friends!

We know that dear friends have an influence on one

another. Jesus calls us friends and indeed teaches us to ask for whatever we want in His name (see John 14:13; 15:15). Catherine demonstrates this key to influencing God's will: intimate friendship with Him.

Shortly after Catherine's father passed away, in October 1370, her mother became dangerously sick. Catherine started praying intensely for her mother's healing. In the process, "the answer she got from heaven was that it would be providential for her mother to die at this time, as this would prevent her from seeing the misfortunes that would otherwise befall her."[61]

Catherine shared with her mother Lapa what the Lord had said and encouraged her to resign herself to this without any sadness. Lapa was horrified. She begged Catherine to go back to the Lord and ask again for her healing. She commanded Catherine never to mention the word "death" again to her.

Catherine went back to prayer and "fervently implored the Lord not to allow her mother to die until she herself was sure that her mother's soul was prepared to do the Divine will."[62] Jesus then communicated to Catherine that he would change his mind and heed her request, not taking Lapa until she was prepared to do His will.

Catherine's mother remained obstinate in paying no attention to her soul, and she died within a short time. Did Catherine get it wrong? Did she not hear God correctly about his promise not to let Lapa die until she was ready to do God's will?

Blessed Raymond described what happened upon Lapa's death, as he and two other witnesses were present.

All three saw Lapa expire after a serious illness lasting many days, saw her inanimate body, and [Catherine] praying, and also clearly heard Catherine's words when

99

she said, "Lord, these are not the promises you made me." After a short time they then saw Lapa's body begin to move and returned to life oh, and all of its members perform their accustomed movements. Of the time she lived after that, there are a whole host of witnesses.[63]

Catherine believed what the Lord said to her about her mother and had faith that was stronger than death. After Catherine declared God's promises, Lapa was raised from the dead. This amazing sign was nothing less than the fruit of her intimacy with Jesus.

7 PROPHETIC MINISTRY TO LEADERS

As Catherine continued to grow in the power and gifts of the Holy Spirit, her favor and influence grew. The stories of her evangelization and supernatural ministry circulated throughout the Church. She was sought for counsel and even served as an ambassador for religious and secular leaders.

It is well known that St. Catherine was instrumental in getting Pope Gregory to move the papacy from Avignon, France, back to Rome. What is not as well known is how she got him to do it.

For decades there had been holy leaders in the Church calling on the popes to move the papacy back to Rome. Almost every pope promised to move back but never followed through. For example, St. Bridget of Sweden put major pressure on Pope Clement VI to return to Rome. She prophetically proclaimed that great suffering and humiliation would come upon the Church if he did not. This warning had no effect on Clement VI or his successor. The papal seat remained in Avignon, and the conflict and division in the Church continued.

What was different about Catherine's approach?

Pope Gregory invited Catherine to visit him in Avignon. He had spoken about eventually moving back to Rome, as had every pope before him, but made no concrete plans to do so. Pope Gregory was well aware of the tension about maintaining the papacy in Avignon. During his time with Catherine, he asked what she thought about the situation.

> "Who knows God's will so well as your holiness, for have you not bound yourself by a vow?" [Catherine replied]. Greatly shaken, Gregory stared at the young woman. He had made a vow that he would return to Rome if he was ever chosen to be Pope. It was while he was still a cardinal. But he had never told a living soul.[64]

In his First Letter to the Corinthians, St. Paul explains that prophetic ministry is powerful because "the secrets of [a person's] heart are disclosed" (1 Corinthians 14:25, RSVCE). Catherine utilized the gift of prophecy with the leader of the universal Church, revealing the secret of the pope's heart regarding the previous vow he had made. This opened the door to heaven's influence in his life.

Convinced of God's presence in the situation through Catherine, Pope Gregory asked her what he needed to do. Now that she had Gregory's attention, Catherine directed him to leave Avignon immediately. Not only did this word of knowledge convict his heart but it imparted the grace to respond. Catherine departed from Avignon, and Pope Gregory abandoned the papal palace within two days. He left for Rome, leaving behind all but six cardinals.

Catherine's prophetic word not only moved the papacy back to Rome but also jump-started a very close friendship between her and Pope Gregory.

St. Catherine, pray for us!

CHAPTER FIVE

ST. FRANCIS XAVIER

CONTEXT AND OVERVIEW

Born to Spanish nobility on April 7, 1506, Francis Xavier exchanged the pursuit of worldly ambitions for advancing the kingdom of God among nations and people groups completely new to the Gospel. He has gone down in history as arguably the most successful missionary, bringing tens of thousands of people into the kingdom of God. He was instrumental in establishing the Church in India, the Malay Archipelago, and Japan.

Just to give you an initial insight into the level of fruit through his ministry, consider the following from one of his letters:

As to the numbers who become Christians, you may understand them from this, that it often happens to me to be hardly able to use my hands from the fatigue of baptizing: often in a single day I have baptized whole villages. Sometimes I have lost my voice and strength altogether with repeating again and again the Credo and the other forms.[65]

St. Francis Xavier has been of great significance and importance in my life, since I chose him to be my Confirmation saint when I was fourteen. It has been said that "no one chooses their confirmation saint; the saint chooses you." This could not be truer for me. As God has transformed my heart and increased my hunger for mission, I have found continued inspiration from the life of St. Francis Xavier.

St. Francis wrote a series of letters detailing his missionary journeys. These will serve as the primary source for what we can receive from the saint.

The fact that Francis ministered to people who had never heard the Gospel increases his importance for us. As the world continues in its slide away from the foundations of Christendom, we can expect to meet people in our spheres of influence who have never heard of Jesus or His Gospel. There is much faith, wisdom, and inspiration that we can receive from Francis Xavier in evangelizing those who are completely new to the Gospel.

THE *ENCOUNTER*
SPIRITUAL EXERCISES AND SURRENDER

Francis Xavier attended the University of Paris, where he roomed with another young man, Peter Faber. When they were both twenty-four, they received a new roommate: Ignatius of Loyola, the future saint and founder of the Society of Jesus, better known as the Jesuit order.

Ignatius was thirty-eight when he arrived as a student. He had experienced a profound conversion as a soldier wounded when a cannonball struck his leg during a battle in Spain. Ignatius ended up forsaking his worldly pursuits and sought to become great in the kingdom of God.

Ignatius made a long spiritual retreat, living in a cave outside Manresa, Spain. It was here that he received revelation from God for the Spiritual Exercises. Just as the military required its soldiers to engage in basic combat training and military exercises, these spiritual exercises would be a means of forming men and women in great faith and intimacy with Jesus.

Ignatius continually witnessed his personal faith in Jesus to Peter Faber and Francis Xavier. Peter Faber would listen, but Francis Xavier would respond with self-protecting sarcasm. Francis had the whole world before him. He was intelligent, athletic, and handsome; and he had many opportunities to serve in high positions and offices after his studies.

Ignatius knew all too well the emptiness of such ambitions. He had a particular heart for Francis Xavier. Ignatius started routinely asking him the famous question posed by Jesus in the Gospel: "Hey, Francis Xavier, what does it profit a man to gain the whole world but lose his soul?" (see Mark 8:36). This question would cause Francis to examine his ambitions and life direction.

Ignatius eventually invited Francis Xavier to experience his Spiritual Exercises, and Francis agreed. Although we do not have particular details of what transpired over those thirty days, we know that Francis Xavier experienced a series of profound encounters with God. These led him not only to fully surrender his life to the service of the kingdom of God but to join the newly formed Jesuit order. He and Peter Faber were among the first seven men to join the Jesuits.

How did God call Francis Xavier to become a world-changing missionary? Was it through a mystical encounter? No. It was the fruit of the surrender he made to God during the Spiritual Exercises and the vows he made to the Society of Jesus.

The king of Portugal requested two Jesuits to minister to a new colony in India. Ignatius chose Simon Rodriguez and Nicholas Bobadilla for the mission. As their time of departure drew near, Bobadilla became sick. He was in no condition to make the voyage, and there was no pausing the voyage to wait for his recovery. Ignatius turned to Francis Xavier and asked him to take his place.

HE HAD NO TRAINING FOR FOREIGN MISSIONS, BUT HE HAD JESUS. JESUS IS ENOUGH.

Francis immediately accepted the mission, without any preparation, and he soon departed for India. His missionary call was a simple matter of surrender and obedience. He had no training for foreign missions, but he had Jesus. Jesus is enough.

MINISTRY LESSONS

1 IDENTIFYING OPPORTUNITIES FOR SUPERNATURAL SIGNS

In one of Francis Xavier's earliest letters, sent shortly after arriving in India, he told Ignatius about his work at his first location, in Goa, India. There had already been some initial evangelization in Goa. Francis Xavier found some early converts and even a newly formed seminary. He asked the seminarians to take him to the villages where the Gospel had already been accepted. On this first mission, he built up these Christians in the faith and ministered to their spiritual needs as well as he could.

After leaving one of the Christian villages, he came upon a village where the local chief had forbidden anyone to convert to Christianity. These people needed a breakthrough. Francis Xavier was informed that a pregnant woman had been in labor for three days and was in danger of dying. Many people were praying to their Hindu gods, and their prayers were having no effect.

Upon hearing this news, Francis recognized an opportunity to minister. He made his way to the woman's house with a translator.

> I went, with one of my companions, to the sick woman's house, and began with confidence to call upon the Name of the Lord, forgetting that I was in a strange land. I thought of that text, "The earth is the Lord's and the fulness thereof, the compass of the world and all that

dwell therein." So I began, through an interpreter, to explain to her the articles of our religion; and by the mercy of God, this woman believed what we taught her. At last I asked her whether she wished to be a Christian. She replied that she would, and gladly. Then I recited a Gospel over her—it was the first time, I suppose, that such words had been heard in those countries. I duly gave her Baptism. Now, to make a long story, immediately after Baptism this good soul, who had put her hope in Christ, and believed, was delivered of her child; and I afterwards baptized her husband, his children, the infant (on the day of its birth), and all the family.[66]

There is much to unpack here. First, although Francis knew that he was in non-Christian territory, he recalled the truth of Psalm 24 that the whole earth is the Lord's. There is no such thing as Christian and non-Christian territory. There is Christian territory and territory that has not been claimed yet for Christ. Francis was set on claiming this territory for the kingdom of God.

I have heard many modern missionaries say that they cannot get to the point of actually sharing the Gospel with non-Christian populations until they gain some level of trust, a process that they claim can take years. Francis Xavier, in his first visit to this village, boldly evangelized in the midst of a need.

Second, Francis Xavier had great faith for healing in the context of the preaching of the Gospel. After Jesus commissioned the disciples and ascended to heaven, "they went forth and preached everywhere, while the Lord worked with them and confirmed the word through accompanying signs" (Mark 16:20). Francis Xavier always put the Gospel first. Although he knew that the woman in labor could be healed, his first priority was to bring health to her soul, which comes from accepting Jesus.

For some Christians, the thought of preaching the Gospel before praying for healing may feel awkward. If you feel awkward about sharing the Gospel message and inviting people to respond to it, just remember this story! It and many others have convinced me to always incorporate the preaching of the Gospel when I have opportunities to pray for healing, both to large groups and in one-on-one situations.

From the time of the early Church, the response to receiving Jesus has not been simply praying a prayer of faith. Although that is very important, Baptism is essential to the response of faith. Francis baptized the woman, and from this she delivered the baby. She and her family acknowledged this as a miracle, and all came to faith. There would soon be a ripple effect:

> The whole village was soon full of the news of the miracle which God had wrought in that house. I went to the chiefs and bade them in the Name of God to acknowledge His Son Jesus Christ, in Whom alone the salvation of all mortals is placed. They said they could not venture to leave the religion of their ancestors without the permission of their master. Then I went to the steward of this chief, who happened to be there to exact some taxes due to his lord. When he had heard me speak about religion, he declared that he thought it a good thing to be a Christian, and that he gave leave to all who liked it to embrace the religion of Jesus Christ. But though he gave this good advice to others he did not practise it himself. However, the chief people of the place, with their whole households, were the first to embrace the faith, the rest followed their example, and so all, of every class and every age, received Baptism. This

work done, we went straight to Tuticorin. The people there received us very kindly, and we have begun to hope that we shall reap an abundant harvest of souls in these parts.[67]

St. Francis Xavier demonstrates the perennial efficacy that signs, wonders, and miracles have in providing breakthrough to those who are not initially open to the Gospel.

2 EQUIPPING & COMMISSIONING CHILDREN FOR HEALING MINISTRY

In his ministry on earth, Jesus continually pointed to the importance of children in the kingdom of God. Consider these two passages:

- "See that you do not despise one of these little ones, for I say to you that their angels in heaven always look upon the face of my heavenly Father" (Matthew 18:10).
- "Let the children come to me and do not prevent them; for the kingdom of God belongs to such as these. Amen, I say to you, whoever does not accept the kingdom of God like a child will not enter it" (Luke 18:16-17).

We can be tempted to limit the meaning of these passages to the qualities of faith and trust that children naturally have toward their parents. However, Jesus makes the bold claim that the kingdom of God actually belongs to children! Children who receive Jesus do not receive a miniature or partial Holy Spirit. They are highly valued and capable members of the kingdom of God. This was Jesus' approach to children in the kingdom. St. Francis Xavier shared it.

Francis equipped children and commissioned them to do ministry—not only as catechists and teachers but as healing evangelists as well. In his letter to Ignatius, Francis Xavier described the overwhelming demand for prayer for the sick and his call for children to participate.

> For my part I desired to satisfy all, both the sick who came to me themselves, and those who came to beg on the part of others, lest if I did not, their confidence in, and zeal for, our holy religion should relax, and I thought it wrong not to do what I could in answer to their prayers. But the thing grew to such a pitch that it was impossible for me myself to satisfy all, and at the same time to avoid their quarrelling among themselves, every one striving to be the first to get me to his own house; so I hit on a way of serving all at once. As I could not go myself, I sent round children whom I could trust in my place. They went to the sick persons, assembled their families and neighbours, recited the Creed with them, and encouraged the sufferers to conceive a certain and well-founded confidence of their restoration. Then after all this, they recited the prayers of the Church. To make my tale short, God was moved by the faith and piety of these children and of the others, and restored to a great number of sick persons health both of body and soul. How good He was to them! He made the very disease of their bodies the occasion of calling them to salvation, and drew them to the Christian faith almost by force![68]

Earlier we saw how effective Francis Xavier was in proclaiming the Gospel and praying for healing, which led to a ripple effect of salvation for an entire village. Francis Xavier did not see this as a one-time glory story. This was a strategy! It was so effective that he equipped and commissioned children to do likewise. Apparently this practice of equipping and involving the youth in healing evangelization was so fruitful that, as I read his letters to other missionaries, he exhorted them to follow it.

Francis Xavier indicates that he used the Apostles' Creed as the basis for the Gospel proclamation. Although he does not share the specifics, he taught the children to bring a sick person to a "well-founded confidence of their restoration." In other words, he taught them how to build an atmosphere of faith and the expectation that people could be healed in that moment. Francis knew that effective healing ministry was not the result of some magic prayer. Rather, healing flowed through faith.

In most accounts of individuals coming to Jesus for healing, He would acknowledge their personal faith in His ability to heal them, even indicating that their healing was made possible through their personal faith. Anyone who is serious about effective healing ministry should pay attention here. Before any prayer, effort should be made to lead people to a place of confidence that Jesus can heal them right then and there. If you don't know how to do that, consider utilizing the Apostles' Creed with an invitation for them to respond, just as Francis Xavier and the children did.

Francis goes on to talk about the incredible fruit of multitudes of people being healed in both body and soul. He had a renewed mind about sickness. For him diseases were not fear-inducing problems but miracles waiting to happen. When we think with the mind of Christ about sickness and healing, we shift from a victim mentality to a victor mentality.

Francis' example of equipping and commissioning children in healing ministry profoundly impacted me. As I was stepping out in greater faith to pray for healing, I started equipping and coaching my children to pray for and see God heal. I don't have time to go into the whole training process, but it was very similar to what we teach at the Encounter School of Ministry, packaged in a way that was accessible to children.

Early in the process, my son Joseph and I met a completely blind woman waiting for her ride outside our local library. Joseph was only about nine years old at the time, and the woman was in her sixties. She wore sunglasses and carried a white cane.

After striking up a conversation and getting to know this woman a bit, I told her that my son and I are Christians, that we belong to a church that prays for healing, and that we have seen God do incredible miracles through very simple prayers. We offered to pray for her to be able to see. She agreed.

Joseph and I prayed for her, then we checked with her, and she said she couldn't see anything but felt the presence of God. We continued to pray, and I was blown away at the level of faith in which Joseph was praying. We checked in after this prayer, and she excitedly described how she could see light and Joseph's outline in front of her. We praised God together! Her vision was starting to improve! The healing had begun.

We explained to the woman that healings can be progressive and that God loves to finish what He starts. We sealed the prayer in Jesus' name and went forth celebrating.

Joseph later told me how helpful it was for me to be there and to facilitate the prayer process. He was thankful that I was there. The truth is, his simple, childlike faith in Jesus strengthened and helped me more than I helped him!

At our Encounter Conference the following year, one of our leaders, Fr. Patrick Gonyeau, was leading a kids' track session. He was teaching the kids about healing prayer in one of the convention center ballrooms. At the same time, Fr. Mathias was leading a healing service for the adults in the main hall. I stopped in to check on what was happening with Fr. Patrick, and what I saw blew my mind.

Fr. Patrick taught the children a very simple way to pray with great faith. Then kids with any kind of physical limitations or pain issues received prayer from other kids. One after another, these beautiful children came up and shared testimonies of restoration and healing. I was so moved by what God was doing through them that, at the end of their session, I had the children come into the adult session. When their corporate healing service was ending and there was an opportunity for individual prayer, we had the children form circles to pray for adults. Any adults still in need of healing were invited to come into one of the circles and receive healing prayer from the children.

To this day, the resulting healing testimonies were some of the most profound and miraculous Encounter Ministries has witnessed. One adult participant, Angel, had stage-4 esophageal cancer. She experienced the healing presence of God through the prayer of a group of children. Later a scan showed that the tumor was gone!

At the conference we had to deal with an emerging problem: adults trying to sneak into the kids' track area to be prayed for! What an awesome problem!

3 THE POWER OF THE GOSPEL MESSAGE

At Encounter Ministries, we are very passionate about the role of signs, wonders, miracles, and healings in the evangelization efforts of the Church. At the same time, we have become aware that when we emphasize amazing testimonies of miracles and healings, some people can think that unless they have the opportunity for some kind of supernatural ministry, they can't effectively evangelize. This is a very serious error.

St. Paul boldly proclaimed, "I am not ashamed of the gospel. It is the power of God for the salvation of everyone who believes" (Romans 1:16). The Gospel message itself is powerful. Yes, we should always be on the lookout for opportunities to supernaturally demonstrate the Gospel, but we need to have our confidence in the Gospel message. Francis Xavier demonstrated this.

In Xavier's evangelization in India, most of the people to whom he ministered were practicing Hinduism. This religion is essentially a form of polytheism. It teaches reincarnation and a caste system, with a religious ruling caste called Brahmins. In his second letter in 1543, Francis Xavier shares about going to one of the Hindu temples, called a pagoda, to evangelize the leaders:

> One day lately, I happened to enter a pagoda where there were about two hundred of them, and most of them came to meet me. We had a long conversation, after which I asked them what their gods enjoined them in order to obtain the life of the blessed. There was a long discussion amongst them as to who should answer me. At last, by common consent, the commission was given to one of them, of greater age and experience than the rest, an old man, of more than eighty years. He asked me in return, what commands the God of the

Christians laid on them. I saw the old man's perversity, and I refused to speak a word till he had first answered my question. So he was obliged to expose his ignorance, and replied that their gods required two duties of those who desired to go to them hereafter, one of which was to abstain from killing cows, because under that form the gods were adored; the other was to show kindness to the Brahmins, who were the worshippers of the gods. This answer moved my indignation, for I could not but grieve intensely at the thought of the devils being worshipped instead of God by these blind [people], and I asked them to listen to me in turn. Then I, in a loud voice, repeated the Apostles' Creed and the Ten Commandments. After this I gave in their own language a short explanation, and told them what Paradise is, and what Hell is, and also who they are who go to Heaven to join the company of the blessed, and who are to be sent to the eternal punishments of hell. Upon hearing these things they all rose up and vied with one another in embracing me, and in confessing that the God of the Christians is the true God.[69]

There are two incredible lessons here. First, Francis Xavier demonstrates practical wisdom. Although he has no interest in learning about Hinduism, he uses the question to create an open door to discussion of salvation in Jesus. As the Hindu leaders explain what it takes to be blessed in the Hindu system, Francis sees a natural place for him to share the Christian answer to the same question.

Effective evangelization requires an open door and a genuine search for the truth on the part of the recipient. When you encounter someone from a different religion (or no religion at all), a great strategy is to ask them basic questions about their core beliefs and to genuinely listen and demonstrate understanding. After they share their beliefs, it is only natural to share with them what you believe, the Gospel message.

At the Encounter School of Ministry, in our quarter on power evangelization, we ensure that all our students are equipped to present the basic Gospel message in a short amount of time and with great confidence. We also provide multiple opportunities for them to do so. Students are often surprised at people's responses to the Gospel message and to the invitation to accept Jesus. Our graduates routinely share that this was one of the most fruitful abilities they acquired during their time at the Encounter School.

Although Xavier's letter does not give details about his Gospel proclamation, we know that it involved explanations of the Creed, the Ten Commandments, and the ultimate realities of heaven and hell. The result of his exposition was that these listeners were convicted of the truth and declared their belief in the Gospel! As St. Paul declared, the Gospel is powerful!

How can we more deeply understand this effect? I believe one of the best insights comes from John 16. There Jesus says that when the Holy Spirit comes, "he will convict the world in regard to sin and righteousness and condemnation: sin, because they do not believe in me" (John 16:8-9).

Although there are many elements involved in sin, Jesus indicates here that the Holy Spirit will convict people of unbelief in Him. This is good news. When we share the Gospel message with someone who does not believe in Jesus, we can expect the Holy Spirit to be present in their hearts, convicting them of the truth of what we are sharing. That means that it is not our job to convict! The Holy Spirit himself convicts people of their unbelief in Jesus.

This is what happened when Francis visited the pagoda. The Holy Spirit came upon the Hindu leaders, convincing them that what they were hearing from Francis Xavier was true. They responded to the Holy Spirit with great faith, accepted Jesus, and started their journey with Him.

So we learn from St. Francis Xavier's example that it's our job to share the Gospel of Jesus Christ; it's the Holy Spirit's role to convict the listener of the truth. But unless we share, no one will be convicted.

4 EQUIPPING TRANSFORMED PEOPLE TO TRANSFORM PEOPLE

When we are asked the "what" of Encounter Ministries--what is our ultimate purpose for a two-year school of ministry---we often respond with one of our favorite sayings: **transformed people transform people**. We all have a sphere of influence. At Encounter we believe that perhaps the greatest key to advancing the kingdom is transforming people so that they can go back and transform others in their spheres of influence.

How is this principle connected to the ministry lessons of Francis Xavier? It was essential in his strategy for evangelizing the people of Japan.

Francis Xavier's success in Japan looked very different from his success in India. When he arrived in India, the Church was already present in nascent form. Christians there experienced the support and protection of the Portuguese colony. In Japan, there was no European colony, and there were no Christians to help Francis.

In his letters of 1548 to the Jesuits in Rome, Francis Xavier recounted how he first learned about Japan. Portuguese merchants told him stories about how educated and learned the people were and about their hunger for knowledge. It was through these merchants that Francis Xavier was first connected to a Japanese citizen named Anger.[70]

Anger's backstory is incredible. He was engaged in a passionate dispute with a fellow countryman and ended up killing this man in a fight. It was not uncommon in Japan to have fights to the death over issues of honor. Anger fled his inland home city and went to a port city. It was there that he met the early Portuguese merchants who recently had started trading in Japan.

Plagued by guilt over the man he had killed, Anger joined these merchants on their voyage to India. He learned Portuguese from them, and these merchants eventually connected him with Francis Xavier, who recounts this story:

> A certain Japanese came to me with this merchant. His name is Anger, and he had made up his mind to come and talk to me, from what he had heard from the people at Malacca. In Japan he had consulted some Portuguese merchants, his friends, and had laid open to them the wounds of his conscience, asking them for some remedy to heal his soul and appease God. These merchants had advised him to come to me at Malacca. . . . He has some knowledge of Portuguese, so we conversed together without an interpreter. If the rest of the Japanese have the same ardour for gaining knowledge that Anger has, then they surpass in genius all nations anywhere found. He was present at the explanation of the Catechism, and with the greatest accuracy wrote down in a book the articles of the Creed. Often, too, in the church, with all the people present, he repeated from memory the lessons he had learned, and asked many questions full of intelligence. In truth, he has a great thirst for knowledge — a

thing which avails very much for a quick perception of truth.[71]

Anger was the first Japanese person Francis Xavier was able to evangelize. Xavier saw in him the potential for an entire people group to receive the Gospel. Francis determined to take Anger under his wing and prepare him to join the mission of bringing the Gospel to his people.

> Anger will learn Portuguese thoroughly; he will become well acquainted with the resources of the Portuguese, the arts of Europe, and our manner of life; he will prepare himself duly for baptism, and will work for me in translating into Japanese the Catechism and a detailed explanation of the history of Christ, since he writes Japanese very well.[72]

After Anger's Baptism, Francis Xavier took him through the Spiritual Exercises, just as Ignatius had done for him. Anger would eventually take the name 'Paul of the Holy Faith.'

After his transformation in Christ, Paul, along with Francis Xavier and a group of missionaries from India, set sail for the first mission to Japan. In Francis' letters back to the Society in Goa, he recounts that it was the ministry of Paul that brought forth the greatest conversions:

> Paul indeed has diligently preached the Gospel day and night to some relations and friends, and has thus brought to the faith of Christ his wife and daughter, as well as many kinsmen and intimate friends. And, as far as things have gone as yet, those who become Christians do not find themselves commonly blamed for what they

have done. As the Japanese for the most part know how to read, they soon learn our prayers by heart.[73]

In later letters to the Society at Goa, Xavier wrote that over a hundred people from Paul's sphere of influence became the first group of converts in Japan. Paul would pastor this community and continue to evangelize the region. In Japan it was not Francis Xavier who did the work of direct evangelization. It was primarily those he raised up and discipled who went forth and helped expand the kingdom. As God equips us, we should seek opportunities to see those we evangelize equipped to advance the kingdom of God in their spheres of influence.

5 THE POWER OF TESTIMONY

One common question that everyone involved in ministry has to answer is, to what degree should I share testimonies and reports about the good things God is doing through me to advance the kingdom of God? Should we keep all our good works secret? Should we actively draw attention to them? This question is very significant, and the subject goes back to Jesus in the Gospels.

On the one hand, Matthew 23 Jesus issues a chapter-long rebuke to the scribes and Pharisees, partly because "they do all their deeds to be seen by men" (Matthew 23:5, RSVCE). The intention behind the Pharisees' good works was to receive the praise of other people. On the other hand, Jesus taught his disciples, "Let your light so shine before men, that they may see your good works and give glory to your Father who is in heaven" (Matthew 5:16, RSVCE).

Although these seem to be contradictory teachings, they are not. The difference is in the intention of the person sharing. The Pharisees were rebuked for wanting their good deeds to be seen by men, and Jesus indicated that they received the reward they sought, the good opinion of others. In Matthew 5, the intention is for our heavenly Father to be glorified. In this case our sharing is of great virtue and bears much fruit.

Through his letters, St. Francis Xavier had the boldness to share with the broader Church the testimonies of what God was doing through his missions. In fact, these mission testimonies inspired countless young men to give their lives to God and pursue ministry in foreign missions. Our very own St. Philip Neri admitted that he was so inspired in reading Xavier's testimonies that he considered leaving his ministry in Rome to join the Jesuits in their foreign missions.

When shared from a heart desiring only the glory of the Father, our testimony of what God has done through us has the power to multiply His grace operating in us. Revelation 19:10 says that "the testimony of Jesus is the spirit of prophecy" (RSVCE). Testimony is essentially related to what Jesus has done in the past; prophecy is directed toward what He wants to do in the future. This Scripture passage links testimony to prophecy: when we share about what Jesus has done in the past, that sharing can release the grace for Jesus to do it again! So, when young men read copies of Francis Xavier's letters, a grace was released on many of them, allowing God to do in them what he did in Xavier.

> SO, WHEN YOUNG MEN READ COPIES OF FRANCIS XAVIER'S LETTERS, A GRACE WAS RELEASED ON MANY OF THEM, ALLOWING GOD TO DO IN THEM WHAT HE DID IN XAVIER.

Francis Xavier made one of the most profound appeals to those back home in a letter to Ignatius. As you read the following, allow Xavier's passion to convict your heart:

> There is now in these parts a very large number of persons who have only one reason for not becoming Christian, and that is that there is no one to make them Christians. It often comes into my mind to go round all the Universities of Europe, and especially that of Paris, crying out every where like a madman, and saying to all the learned men there whose learning is so much greater than their charity, "Ah! what a multitude of souls is through your fault shut out of heaven and falling into hell!" Would to God that these men who labour so much in gaining knowledge would give as much thought to the account they must one day give to God of the use they have made of their learning and of the talents entrusted to them! I am sure that many of them would be moved by such considerations, would exercise themselves in fitting meditations on Divine truths, so as to hear what God might say to them, and then, renouncing their ambitions and desires, and all the things of the world, they would form themselves wholly according to God's desire and choice for them. They would exclaim from the bottom of their hearts: "Lord, here am I; send me whithersoever it shall please Thee, even to India!"[74]

Imagine being a young man and reading about the preaching, the miracles, and the multitudes accepting Jesus, then reading an appeal that encourages you to reap a harvest! Francis understood the vanities of the world. He overcame them, and he spoke with great authority of how much greater it is to live for the kingdom of God than to live for the kingdom of the world:

> Good God! how much happier and how much safer they would be! With what far greater confidence in God's mercy would they meet their last hour, the supreme trial of that terrible judgment which no man can escape! They would then be able joyfully to use the words of the faithful servant in the Gospel: "Lord, Thou gavest me five talents; behold, I have gained beside them other five!" They labour night and day in acquiring knowledge; and they are very diligent indeed in understanding the subjects which they study; but if they would spend as much time in that which is the fruit of all solid learning, and be as diligent in teaching to the ignorant the things necessary to salvation, they would be far better prepared to give an account of themselves to our Lord when He shall say to them: "Give an account of thy stewardship." Fear much that these men, who spend so many years in the Universities in studying the liberal arts, look more to the empty honours and dignities of the prelature than to the holy functions and obligations of which those honours are the trappings. It has come to this pass, as I see, that the men who are the most diligent in the higher branches of study, commonly make profession that they hope to gain some high post in the Church by their reputation for learning, therein to be able to serve our Lord and His Church. But all the time they deceive themselves miserably, for their studies are far more directed to their own advantage than to the common good.[75]

St. Francis Xavier inspired a generation of disciples to respond to God's call to go to the nations and participate in the great commission. He effectively utilized the power of testimony through his letters and was effective in calling young men out of the emptiness of worldly pursuits and into a greater surrender to God's will. Countless men and women would follow in his footsteps to bring the light of the Gospel into the darkest places of the world. Jesus is still calling his disciples to follow Him into the nations to advance the kingdom with the power of the Holy Spirit.

St. Francis Xavier, pray for us!

CHAPTER SIX

ST. PADRE PIO

CONTEXT AND OVERVIEW

Francesco Forgione was born in the small Italian town of Pietrelcina, Italy, on May 25, 1887. . He would become the great St. Padre Pio, one of the most supernaturally charged saints of the twentieth century. At his canonization, the Church declared, "He was always immersed in supernatural realities. Not only was he himself a man of hope and total trust in God, but by word and example he communicated these virtues to all who approached him."[76]

Padre Pio manifested and ministered in the gifts of the Holy Spirit—including healing, miracles, prophecy, words of knowledge, discernment of Spirits, varieties of tongues, and interpretation of tongues. Padre Pio even experienced the grace of bilocation beyond the walls of his friary in San Giovani Rotundo.

To this day, there are countless testimonies of people who received life-changing supernatural ministry through Padre Pio. While God called St. Francis Xavier to be set on fire to spread the Gospel to the nations, God called Padre Pio to be on fire in the simple Franciscan friary in San Giovanni Rotundo, and from there the nations came to Padre Pio.

The light that shone through Padre Pio was so great and transformative that his ministry would attract thousands of pilgrims from across the world every year. People wanted to experience the gifts that he made available to everyone he met and ministered to. These included the future St. John Paul II, who made a confession to Padre Pio and allegedly received a prophecy of his future pontificate.

Although Padre Pio ministered powerfully in the gifts of the Holy Spirit, a unique lesson we can receive from him is the way he involved his guardian angel in ministry. In fact, it can be argued that no one has done more than Padre Pio to renew our mind about our capacity to involve our angels in ministry. Padre Pio's partnership with his angel profoundly impacted his ministry.

It is important to understand that Padre Pio's interaction with his guardian angel was never intended to showcase a special gift that only he could enjoy. Padre Pio saw this partnering as a way for all faithful Christians to activate angelic assistance.

THE *ENCOUNTER*
EARLY VISIONS

Although a poor farming family, the Forgiones were very rich in the life of the Spirit. Padre Pio committed his life to Jesus at the age of five, and he developed a strong life of prayer throughout his childhood. He modeled the childlike faith that Jesus spoke of and thus received the kingdom of God. He had spiritual conversations with Jesus, Mary, and his guardian angel. For Padre Pio, the supernatural was natural. Such a worldview, when properly understood, is the Catholic worldview.

Regarding the outpouring of the Holy Spirit, St. Peter the apostle quoted the prophet Joel: "Your young men shall see visions" (Acts 2:17; Joel 3:1). Although we do not know their exact content, we do know that Padre Pio experienced divine visions; the invisible realm of the Spirit was open to him. During childhood Francesco had vivid encounters with the angel assigned to him. He would later recount that he assumed every young Christian had these encounters.

At the age of sixteen, Francesco entered the Capuchin Order of the Friars Minor novitiate. When he was twenty-three, he was ordained to the priesthood, taking the name Pio. He was affectionately called Padre Pio.

Padre Pio's ministry and connection with his angel cannot be properly understood without an understanding of the immense suffering of love he experienced. He had a devotion to the passion and suffering of Jesus. Early in his priesthood, he hungered for greater participation in this suffering.

> Like the Apostle Paul, Padre Pio da Pietrelcina placed at the centre of his life and apostolic work the Cross of his Lord as his strength, his wisdom and his glory. Inflamed by love of Jesus Christ, he became like him in the sacrifice of himself for the salvation of the world. In his following and imitation of the Crucified Christ he was so generous and perfect that he could have said: "I have been crucified with Christ; it is no longer I who live, but Christ who lives in me" (Gal 2:20).[77]

Jesus heard Padre Pio's prayer for unity with and participation in his suffering. When the priest was thirty-one years old, he had a life-changing encounter with Jesus while praying in front of a crucifix after offering Mass. In that encounter, he received the stigmata, the wounds of Christ in his hands, feet, and side. Padre Pio thus entered deeply into the mystery of the suffering of Jesus. This in turn released increased power in his ministry. Padre Pio bore the stigmata for his fifty remaining years.

It was in this context that God taught Padre Pio about the potential of partnering with angels in ministry, to have a greater spiritual impact.

MINISTRY LESSONS

1 FAITH TO RELEASE ANGELS IN MINISTRY

In order to receive the ministry lessons of Padre Pio's partnership with the angels, we must first have a proper theological view about the role of the angels and our relationship with them.

At Mass each week, we profess belief in the reality of both the visible and the invisible realms. Consider the opening words of the Nicene Creed: "I believe in one God, the Father almighty, maker of heaven and earth, of all things visible and invisible." The invisible spiritual realm is just as real as the visible.

Of all the realities in the invisible realm, angels dominate. Consider the following:

- In the Old Testament, there are 114 references to angels. In the New Testament, there are 179 such references.
- Jesus said to his disciples, "Take care that you do not despise one of these little ones; for, I tell you, in heaven their angels continually see the face of my Father in heaven" (Matthew 18:10, NRSVCE). Each person has been assigned at least one angel to minister to them.
- Psalm 91:11 says, "For he commands his angels with regard to you, to guard you wherever you go."

God has assigned angels to help us stay in alignment with Him. Although we traditionally refer to them as our guardian angels, they do much more than assist in our protection.

Although most Christians acknowledge the presence of an angel assigned to their life, there is often misunderstanding about the type of relationship we can have with our angels. To what degree can we expect to interact with them?

Let's look to the Book of Hebrews for a clear scriptural basis for our answer: "Are they not all ministering spirits sent forth to serve (*diakonia*), for the sake of those who are to obtain salvation?" (Hebrews 1:14, RSVCE).

The term "ministering spirits" is a direct reference to our angels. Their job is to serve those who are to obtain salvation. Who is to obtain salvation? We are! In what way should we expect the angels' service?

The Greek word from which we translate the verb

"to serve" is *diakonia*. According to *Strong's Exhaustive Concordance of the Bible*, the definition of *diakonia* is "service, ministering, esp. of those who execute the commands of others."[78] This kind of service thus involves executing others' commands. We know that the angels execute the commands of God, but this passage indicates that they also serve us and therefore can be expected to some degree to respond to our commands.

What does this look like? Spiritual Doctor and early Church Father St. John Chrysostom said this:

> And so [our angels] are partners in service with us. Consider how he ascribes no great difference to the kinds of creatures. And yet the space between angels and men is great; nevertheless he brings them down near to us, all but saying, For us they labor, for our sake they run to and fro: on us, as one might say, they wait. This is their ministry, for our sake to be sent every way.[79]

The key to understanding our relationship with our angels is knowing that they are assigned to us by God and that we are able to send them. This denotes the authority that God has assigned to us in regard to our angels. Does that mean that we can send angels to do anything we want? Absolutely not. The angels are only assigned to us because we have an assignment from God to advance his kingdom on the earth. To the degree that we are operating in our God-given assignment, we can expect our angels to respond to the assignments we give them.

Not only did Padre Pio understand these theological truths; he actually put them into practice.

2 SENDING ANGELS TO MINISTER

Throughout Padre Pio's life, his angel was something of an extension of his personal ministry when he was not physically able to assist someone. Padre Pio often sent his angel to those in need. To his good friend Padre Benedetto he wrote:

> The Lord knows what tears I shed for you especially since I know what you are suffering. I never begin to pray without presenting you to our most sweet Jesus. I have never ascended the altar without recommending you fervently to the heavenly father. On the 20th of the month, I offered the holy sacrifice for you. My good Guardian Angel knows this and I have entrusted him many times with a delicate task of coming to console you.[80]

This incredible example provides an important theological distinction. Padre Pio comes boldly in intercession to "sweet Jesus" and Abba Father. When we intercede to God, we know that our prayers of intercession are powerful, but ultimately we have no authority in how God responds to our prayer. Our angels, on the other hand, are under our service, and we do have influence over how our angel responds. Padre Pio had great faith in his ability to partner with his angel to bring consolation to his friend.

We should not be surprised when we receive confirmations of angels responding in very direct ways to our leading. Consider the following example.

As Padre Pio advanced in age, he required the help of other friars to execute his duties. One of these helpers was Padre Alessio Parente. Alessio's duties allowed for little rest, so he sometimes suffered extreme fatigue. One of his tasks was to guide Padre Pio through the multitudes at the end of Mass. But because of fatigue, Padre Alessio often slept through his alarm clock, or sometimes he turned it off in his sleep.

Invariably, when the time drew near to assist Padre Pio, Padre Alessio would hear a knock on his door. When he arose to see who it was, nobody was at the door. He would then realize it was time to help Padre Pio. He would arrive just in time.

On one occasion, Padre Alessio slept through the knock as well. He later apologized to Padre Pio, who said to him, "Yes I understand you, but do you think I will continue to send my guardian angel every day to wake you up? You'd better go and buy yourself a new alarm clock."[81]

This last testimony was very impactful for me. In the big picture of life, it really is not a big deal when someone is late or does not respond. The inconvenience that Padre Pio faced from a tardy Padre Alessio may not seem to require supernatural intervention. But in the kingdom of God, that which is important to us is important to our angels. In the kingdom there is no line about when it is OK to send our angels and when it is not.

As a senior leader of Encounter Ministries, I often find myself in situations in which I really need a response from someone but do not want to burden myself (or them) with extensive e-mails and text message reminders. I started entrusting the needed responses to my guardian angel, sending him in faith to prompt the person for a response and then choosing not to worry. I saw an incredible rate of response! Without any prompting on my part, the people to whom I sent my angels started responding to me very promptly. I even started hearing testimonies where people would reply to me and tell me something like, 'I'm so sorry I forgot to respond to you...

I then started getting internal reminders out of nowhere and remembered it was a long time. My apologies for the late response!' The reality is that the reminder did not come from nowhere. I believe it came from my angel.

3 GROWING IN RELATIONSHIP WITH YOUR ANGEL

Opportunities to send our angels to minister on our behalf are abundant. As we grow in our relationships with our angels, we can boldly involve them in our daily lives.

Padre Pio discovered that it is possible to have a personal relationship with one's angel. It was not only faith in his ability to send his angel but also an intimate relationship with his angel that bore great fruit. But although he experienced a close relationship with his angel, it was nowhere close to the level of relationship he had with Jesus. In fact, the only reason Padre Pio was able to have a relationship with his angel is because of his relationship with Jesus.

Was this connection with his angel a special gift for a special priest? No. Padre Pio taught that it was possible for every Christian to cultivate a spiritual relationship with their angel. In a letter to his spiritual daughter Rafaelina Cerase in 1914, he gave her the following counsel:

> Know, O Raffaelina, that this good angel prays for you: he offers to God all your good works that you accomplish, as well as your holy and pure desires. In the hours in which you seem to be alone and abandoned, do not complain about not having a soul-mate to whom you can open (your heart) and to whom you can confide your sorrows: —for the love of God, do not forget this invisible companion who is always present to listen to you and always ready to console you.

> O delightful intimacy, O blessed companionship! Oh, if only all men knew how to understand and appreciate this very great gift that God, in the excess of His love for men, has assigned to us this celestial spirit! Recall frequently his presence: you ought to fix your mind's eye upon him. Thank him, pray to him. He is so finely mannered, so discreet: respect him. Have continual fear lest you offend the purity of his gaze. [82]

Here Padre Pio gives the instruction to open the heart and share the deepest parts of our life with our angel. He indicates that in sharing our thoughts with our angels, we should expect to receive their thoughts as well. What does this look like?

Although Padre Pio did not provide many specific details about the manner in

PADRE PIO TAUGHT THAT IT WAS POSSIBLE FOR EVERY CHRISTIAN TO CULTIVATE A SPIRITUAL RELATIONSHIP WITH THEIR ANGEL.

which he communicated with his angel, evidence reveals that much of his relationship involved a spiritual conversation. This was very similar to the spiritual "colloquies" that St. Ignatius taught his students to engage in through his Spiritual Exercises. The colloquy is "an intimate conversation between you and God the Father, between you and Jesus, or between you and Mary or one of the saints." [83]

The theological basis of the colloquy, and the manner in which we receive all revelation from God, is grounded in 1 Corinthians 2:12-16. St. Paul declares that through the Holy Spirit in us, "we have the mind of Christ." The Holy Spirit fundamentally and eternally changed us when we received Him. That transformation includes transforming our mind and all its faculties, including the interior voice of the mind, our imagination, our thoughts, and so on. Ignatius tells us that the faculties of our mind become the means by which we can receive communication from God and potentially Mary and the communion of saints. Padre Pio expanded this understanding to include the angels as well.

On occasion Padre Pio would actually engage in these conversations out loud. On November 29th, 1911, Fr. Agostino took notes on one of these conversations:

> ... Angel of God, my Angel. ...Are you not taking care of me? ... Are you a creature of God? ...Either you're a creature of God or a creator... You're a Creator? No! Therefore you are God's creature and you have laws which you must obey... You must stay beside me whether you want to or not... He laughs... What is there to laugh about? Tell me one thing... You must tell me... Who was here yesterday morning? ...And he laughs... You must tell me... Who was it? . . . Either Fr. Agostino or the superior... Tell me then... Was it perhaps their secretaries? answer me now... If you don't answer me I will say it was one of those for... He laughs... An angel laughs! ...Tell me then... I won't leave you until you tell me. [84]

Padre Pio had a playful and somewhat teasing relationship with his angel. In this colloquy, he was pressing his angel to essentially give him words of knowledge about who was present the day before. The entire time, he sees his angel laughing, and he laughs in response.

It is interesting to note that this colloquy was recorded in Padre Pio's first year of priesthood, before he was well known for his supernatural ministry. What is clear is that Padre Pio had been cultivating a relationship with his guardian angel throughout his life. In other testimonies, we learn that through his relationship with his guardian angel, he received many words of knowledge in ministry. It is important for us to know that some of the words of knowledge that we receive can come directly through our angels.

At the Encounter School, during our quarter called Advanced Ministry Training, we create space for our students to gain greater faith, awareness, and discernment of the presence of their angel in ministry. Padre Pio sets an amazing example, and he has helped many students unlock a greater relationship with their angel. To date, some of my favorite testimonies from this quarter involve students experiencing greater connection with their guardian angel and increased fruitfulness, not only in ministry situations but in important life decisions.

One priest who went through the Encounter School shared a testimony with us about how he cultivated a life-changing relationship with his angel. Through some of the activation exercises in that quarter, he had a powerful encounter with his angel and started gaining awareness of which inspirations were from his angel and which were from the Holy Spirit. He became aware of the kind of spiritual support he could receive from his angel.

What began in the activation would continue and mature. This priest shared stories of being stuck in ministry situations with people, turning to his angel for support, and getting breakthroughs very quickly. He came to experience the reality that his angel had always been there, and he had not taken advantage of all the ways the angel could help him. He also became aware of the difference between the sound and feel of his guardian angel's voice and the voice of the Holy Spirit. Even greater than the ministry support was the intimacy and heavenly friendship that were stirred up.

It is also worth mentioning that in the course of seeking greater connection with your angel, any revelation you receive must be exercised according to the principles of discernment with the Holy Spirit. Deception and error are possible. Yet Padre Pio had great confidence in our ability to be in right relationship and connection with our angels when we engage with them. A greater error than failing to exercise mature discernment in your connection with your angel would be to not pursue a connection at all!

4 PROPER COMMUNICATION WITH ANGELS

With such closeness and familiarity, we might assume that Padre Pio and his angel were on a first name basis. This is not the case. Upon overhearing another colloquy with his angel the following month, Padre Agostino transcribed the following:

> Angel of Mine... Well done, little child. ... Now, he becomes serious . . . he pouts ... what am I to call you? . . . What is your name? . . .
>
> But you understand, Angel of mine, forgive me, you understand ... Bless Jesus for me.[85]

Here Padre Pio, in spiritual conversation with his angel, attempted to learn his name. Although we don't know exactly how his angel responded, it is clear through Padre Pio's apology that his angel likely rebuked him for seeking this knowledge.

Padre Pio was therefore content with referring to his angel with great intimacy and according to his angel's function, with titles like "my heavenly companion, protector and friend." Padre Pio's example is congruent with the Vatican's Directory on Popular Piety and the Liturgy: "The practice of assigning names to the Holy Angels should be discouraged, except in the cases of Gabriel, Raphael and Michael whose names are contained in Holy Scripture."[86]

I have friends who believe that their angels have revealed their proper names to them. Although this is certainly possible, in obedience we avoid assigning proper names to our angels. We can receive inspiration from the example of Padre Pio, who in his great humility experienced a profound partnership and intimacy with his angel without knowing his angel's name.

5 PROTECTION FROM ATTACK

For our struggle is not with flesh and blood but with the principalities, with the powers, with the world rulers of this present darkness, with the evil spirits in the heavens.
(Ephesians 6:12)

We know that we are at war with the devil and the fallen angels. As we grow into maturity in the spiritual life and work to spread the Gospel, we gain a greater awareness of the various attacks of evil spirits against us. We should have great confidence in the authority that we have in Christ for our protection. How is this to be exercised?

Some Christians, when they become aware of demonic attack, have a tendency to confront the evil spirits one-on-one. They utilize all the deliverance prayers they know as weapons against the enemy. Although this can be effective, it can be incredibly draining and can cause us to be distracted from our divine assignments.

Padre Pio had a different approach to spiritual warfare. One of his letters tells us:

> How consoling it is to know that we are always under the protection of a heavenly spirit, who never abandons us, not even (most admirable fact!) in the very act by which we displease God! How sweet this great truth is for the believing soul! What can the devout soul fear that is diligent in loving Jesus, and that always has such a distinguished fighter present by its side? Oh, was he not perchance among those many who, together with St. Michael the Angel there in the empyreal heights defended the honor of God against Satan and all the other rebellious spirits, finally reducing them to perdition and casting them into hell (see Daniel 10:13; 12:1; Revelation 12:7)?
>
> Well then, know that he is still powerful against Satan and his satellites. His charity has not grown less, nor will it ever fail to protect us. Form the beautiful habit of thinking about him always.[87]

Here Padre Pio presents our angels as distinguished fighters and speculates that our angels were likely present with St. Michael on the day that the devil and the fallen angels were driven out of heaven. Padre Pio advises that, if evil spirits are coming to attack us in the spiritual realm, it makes more sense for us to call upon and send our angel into the fight than to try and fight the battle ourselves. Yes, we are supposed to pray, but we are not the ones who are supposed to do the fighting. Although we can fight the enemy directly in various confrontational prayers, such engagement can wear us out.

Let me give you an example of what this can look

like. During one of the most important seasons of growth for Encounter Ministries, some of my children started having very intense nightmares. The world of dreams has great potential for crossover with the spiritual realm. God often chooses to communicate and connect with us in our dreams. At the same time, evil spirits can attempt to influence the dream realm as well.

I was getting woken up and called frequently into the kids' rooms to minister to them. They would describe the kind of images present, and I could see signs of evil spirits all over the situations. I would go into my spiritual warfare posture and do everything I knew how to do at the time to battle the enemy. I was binding spirits, rebuking them, praying the blood of Jesus, praying in tongues, declaring the promises of God, and more!

IF EVIL SPIRITS ARE COMING TO ATTACK US IN THE SPIRITUAL REALM, IT MAKES MORE SENSE FOR US TO CALL UPON AND SEND OUR ANGEL INTO THE FIGHT THAN TO TRY AND FIGHT THE BATTLE OURSELVES.

Through this prayer, my kids would experience peace and eventually get back to sleep. But there were two unfortunate effects. First, these experiences would wear me out and hurt my rest. Second, my kids developed an expectation that unless Daddy came in and engaged in this spiritual battle, they were powerless.

During this time, I came into a greater revelation about the presence of angels. The next time the nightmares came, I went into the kids' room and gently declared with great faith that the angels God has given them are greater than anything that was stirring up fear. (I intentionally did not reference "demons" or "evil spirits.") I prayed the simple prayer: "Angels, I thank you for your protection, and I entrust the protection of my children tonight completely to you. Thank you for going to war and clearing the spiritual atmosphere of anything that could cause fear. Amen." After that I kissed my children and calmly walked out. There were no more calls for the rest of the week or in the time to come!

A few weeks later, my daughter Gianna came to me in great fear, believing that she saw some kind of skeleton creature in her room. After chatting with her, I came to the conclusion that she really was seeing something, although it was not physical. It seemed as if a demon was manifesting itself to her in the spirit, making her think it was also physical.

Remembering the power of her angel, I asked Gianna to close her eyes and pray, "Jesus, please show me where my guardian angel is right now." After a few moments, in her spirit she saw her angel present with great power. He was binding the skeleton creature with vines from heaven, and then he cast it out. That did it. No more terror.

Jesus taught us, "Everything is possible to one who has faith" (Mark 9:23). When we have faith in the angels whom God has given us and express our faith in partnering with them, we can expect great breakthroughs!

St.Padre Pio, pray for us!

CHAPTER SEVEN

ST. SERAPHIM
OF SAROV

CONTEXT AND OVERVIEW

Up to this point, I have featured saints who lived and ministered in the Western Church. I want to invite you to turn East, to an incredibly transformative saint, Seraphim of Sarov. The best way I have found to describe him to people unfamiliar with his life is that he is like the Padre Pio of eighteenth-and-early-nineteenth-century Russia.

Prokhor Moshnin was born on July 19, 1754, to Isidore and Agathia Moshnin, in Kursk, Russia. At the age of eighteen, Prokhor followed God's call to become a monk and entered the monastery of Sarov. Upon taking vows at the age of twenty-seven, he was given the religious name Seraphim, which in Hebrew means "fiery" or "burning." This name would prove to be prophetic.

Seraphim's life was marked by the burning love of the Holy Spirit. As with Padre Pio, multitudes from across the continent would travel to receive prayer ministry from Seraphim in his humble cell in Sarov. According to Archimandrite Lazarus, "All Russia abounds in tales about the miracles of 'Fr. Seraphim.'"[88] The miracles, signs, and wonders that flowed from his life brought incredible renewal to the Church and the people of God in Russia. Seraphim was not content, however, with being the vessel through which people received God's loving touch. He was passionate about seeing ordinary Christians transformed to be more like Jesus.

The first half of the ministry lessons of this chapter focus on lessons related to wisdom from Seraphim on praying for healing. I will then shift to lessons about cultivating a greater life in the Holy Spirit. These latter lessons are based on a prophetic presentation Seraphim gave, which has come to be known as "On Acquisition of the Holy Spirit."

THE *ENCOUNTER*
CALLED BY MARY

Similar to St. Catherine of Siena, Seraphim would initially pursue the hermetic lifestyle. For him this consisted of solitude, contemplative union with Jesus, and minimal connection with other members of the monastery. All of that would change around the year 1813, an early biography indicates, when Seraphim had a profound encounter with Mary, who was accompanied by St. Onuphrius the Great and St. Peter of Athos.[89] In this encounter, Mary told Seraphim that he was not meant to live in seclusion anymore. God wanted him to start receiving people in his room. Seraphim resolved to open his door to the world.

Soon after this, General Otrostchenkoff and his wife, Natalia, visited the monastery on their way to Moscow. After attending the Divine Liturgy, the couple proceeded to leave a gift at the hermit's door. To their surprise, the door opened, and Seraphim invited them in.

Natalia had poor health, which led to perpetual coughing and vomiting. To make a long story short, she was healed after Seraphim ministered to her. With great joy, the couple went forth sharing their testimony.

This miracle would be the first of countless demonstrations of heaven that flowed through Seraphim's ministry. Christians from all over the region would seek out the saint at the monastery, and no one who came left unchanged. The many testimonies of his ministries as well as the teachings of Seraphim to his fellow monastics give us much wisdom for supernatural ministry.

MINISTRY LESSONS

1 FREEDOM FROM PRESSURE

Fr. Mathias has a great saying about healing ministry: "100 percent of the people you don't pray for do not get healed. Even though not everyone we pray for will be healed, as we pray for more people, we will see more healings."

Encounter students start out praying in the school context, where we have created a safe and responsible environment to begin engaging in healing ministry. Every year we see incredible healings through students' ministry to one another. We have seen a pattern: as a student grows in healing ministry, they step out and pray for close friends and family members in need of healing. God honors their faith, boldness, and obedience, and people get healed. Testimonies go around their sphere of influence, and before they know it, people believe that the student has some kind of unique healing power.

As people start seeking them for healing prayer, students can experience pressure to meet the expectations thrust on them. Often the pressure paralyzes them and renders their ministry more ineffective because they unintentionally put pressure on themselves.

If you can understand or relate to this, then you can learn a lot from how St. Seraphim prayed for healing.

Although there are many healing testimonies attributed to the ministry and intervention of St. Seraphim, only a few of them provide insight into the mindset with which he prayed. In these few accounts, it appears that Seraphim intentionally drew faith in Jesus from the individual and did so in a way that put no pressure on his own role in the healing.

One of the earliest healing testimonies came from a man named Michael Vasilievitch Manturov. While in the army, Michael contracted an incurable disease in his legs. This grew to menacing proportions and involved bits of bones becoming detached and causing him great pain when walking. Upon hearing the testimonies of Seraphim, Manturov came to him for healing. With tears, he begged Seraphim to heal him.

The saint recognized that Manturov was placing his faith in Seraphim and not in God. Seraphim knew that in spite of any spiritual gifts present only God can heal. He also understood that he had a role to play in the process. How did he respond to Manturov?

Father asked him three times with the deepest sympathy and fatherly love: "Do you believe in God?" And having received a thrice-repeated vigorous affirmation of his sincere and absolute faith in God, Saint Seraphim said: "My Joy, if you have such Faith, believe also that to a believer everything is possible through God. And I, poor Seraphim, I shall pray."[90]

It is great if a person has confidence in the person praying, but what is needed is direct faith in God. Seraphim drew out Manturov's faith that God could heal him. In so doing, the pressure to heal was off Seraphim. The only thing that remained was for him to partner with Manturov's faith and pray.

Seraphim then went to his cell to pray, very likely receiving guidance

> "MY JOY, IF YOU HAVE SUCH FAITH, BELIEVE ALSO THAT TO A BELIEVER EVERYTHING IS POSSIBLE THROUGH GOD. AND I, POOR SERAPHIM, I SHALL PRAY."[90]

on how to minister. He came out and anointed Manturov's diseased legs, put a heavy quantity of dry bread into Manturov's coat to weigh him down, and then commanded him to walk to the hostel in town—something that would be impossible without pain. Manturov obeyed and started walking. In the process, he realized that he was walking without any feeling of pain whatsoever and that his legs were firm again!

Now, most people respond to being healed by praising Jesus and then honoring and thanking the person who prayed for them. Manturov skipped any praise to

God and ran back to the monastery, throwing himself at Seraphim's feet and thanking him for the healing. Seraphim rebuked him:

> "What are you thinking of? This is the work of the Lord alone, who does the will of those who fear Him! Give thanks to the Lord Almighty and to His Immaculate Mother!"[91]

God is the one who deserves honor and glory. When a person does not thank God for a healing and attributes the miracle to the person praying, we need to issue correction and make sure that God is glorified.

We can gain wisdom from the way that St. Seraphim helped people put their gaze on Jesus. When the focus is on Jesus, the pressure is off us, and we can more freely respond to the promptings and guidance of the Holy Spirit.

2 FAITH AND PERSEVERANCE FOR HEALING

In praying for healing for our brothers and sisters in Christ, we have perceived an increase of fruitfulness when we identify the faith a person has for their healing. We see this in Acts 14, in which Paul was preaching in Lystra and became aware of a crippled man who was listening. "Paul, looking intently at him and seeing that he had faith to be made well, said in a loud voice, 'Stand upright on your feet.' And he sprang up and walked" (Acts 14:9-10, RSVCE).

St. Seraphim too was aware of what faith for healing looks like in a person. An example of this comes from the personal journal of Nikolas Alexandrovitch Motovilov.

Motovilov was suffering from extremely severe rheumatic pain and paralysis in the legs, which were twisted and swollen at the knees. He also suffered from incurable bed sores on his back and sides. Upon hearing of Seraphim's ministry, he journeyed to Sarov. After two meetings, he had received no healing, but he persevered. On September 9, 1831, five servants carried him to meet again with Seraphim. He recorded in his journal:

> To my request that he should help me and heal me he replied: "But I am not a doctor. One must apply to doctors when one wants to be cured of some illness."

> I told him in detail of my sufferings, of how I had experienced all the main kinds of treatment, without having obtained healing from a single one. And now I saw no other way of salvation and I had no other hope of being healed of my ailments other than the grace of God. But as I was a sinner and had no boldness toward the Lord God, I asked his holy prayers that the Lord should heal me.

> He asked me: "Do you really believe in the Lord Jesus Christ, that he is the God-man, and in the most pure Mother of God, that she is ever–virgin?"

> I replied: "I do."

> "And do you believe," he continued, " that as formerly the Lord healed instantly with one word or by his touch all the diseases which afflict men, so now too, he can heal as easily and instantaneously as before those who ask his help, by a single word of his, and that the prayer of the Mother of God is all-powerful, so that at her intercession the Lord Jesus Christ can even now heal

you completely, in an instant, and by a single word?"

I replied that I truly believed all this, I believed it with all my soul and heart, and that unless I had believed it, I would not have ordered my servants to bring me to him.

Initially Seraphim realized that Motovilov was putting his faith in Seraphim's ability to bring forth his healing, for Motovilov "was a sinner and had no boldness toward the Lord." Here again, Seraphim shifted the focus to Jesus and Jesus' ability to heal. He essentially drew out Motovilov's faith. And just as St. Paul saw the crippled man's faith for healing, Seraphim saw that gift in Motovilov.

" But if you believe," he concluded, "you are already well!"

" How am I well," I asked, "when my servants and you are holding me in your hands?"

" No," he said, "you are completely well now in the whole of your body."

And he told my men, who were holding me in their hands, to leave me; and taking me by the shoulders, he raised me from the ground himself. Then, putting me on my feet, he said to me: "Stand more firmly, fix your feet squarely on the ground, there—like that. Don't be afraid, you are quite well now." And then he added, looking at me joyfully: "There, you see how well you are standing now!"

I replied, "I can't help standing well since you're holding me so firmly and well."

You might feel an uncomfortable cringe as you visualize this scene. The man could not walk. Many people would likely stop their course of ministry at this point. But St. Seraphim picked up the paralyzed man and tried, unsuccessfully, to convince him that he was not paralyzed.

In our experience at Encounter, some major healings have come by not giving up but boldly persevering for the breakthrough. This is what Seraphim did. If he had stopped, Motovilov would not have encountered the healing power of the Holy Spirit. The story continues:

Then he took his hands off me and said: "Well, now I am no longer holding you, and you are still standing firmly even without me. Now walk boldly. The Lord has healed you. So go and move from your place."

Taking me by the arm with one of his hands, and with the other pushing me a little between the shoulders, he led me on the grass and on the rough ground near the big pine trees, saying: "There, [your excellency], how well you walk!"

I replied: "Yes, because you are so kind as to lead me so well."

"No," he said, taking his hand off me. "The Lord himself has been pleased to heal you completely, and the Mother of God herself has prayed to Him about this. Now you will walk without my help and you will always walk well. So walk!" And he began to push me in order to make me walk.

"But I shall fall and hurt myself," I said.

" No," he contradicted me, "you will not hurt yourself, but you will walk firmly."

And when I felt in myself some power from on high overshadowing me, I took courage a little and began to walk firmly.

SOMETIMES HEALING DOES NOT MANIFEST RIGHT AWAY; THE PER-SON NEEDS TO ACTIVATE THEIR FAITH AND DO SOMETHING THEY COULD NOT DO BEFORE THE PRAYER.

Unless you're operating at a high and proven level of prophetic revelation, you should not guarantee a future healing. For Seraphim, in this process of persevering faith, he was inferentially receiving revelation of Mary's intercession and the conviction that Jesus wanted to heal Motovilov right then, even though there was as yet no indication of any healing. That changed when Seraphim directed Motovilov to do something he could not do. Seraphim added a little push for good measure. Once Motovilov started walking, he felt the Holy Spirit overshadow him and enable him to walk.

Sometimes healing does not manifest right away; the person needs to activate their faith and do something they could not do before the prayer. Motovilov's testimony continues:

But he suddenly stopped me, saying: "That is enough now."

Then he asked me: "Well, are you sure now that the Lord has actually healed you, and healed you completely? . . . [A]ccustom yourself to walking little by little, and take care of your health as a precious gift of God."

And he went on talking with me even after this for a considerable time. Then he sent me away to the hostel completely healed. And so my men went back alone from the forest and the near Hermitage to the monastery, thanking God for his wonderful mercies to me which have been displayed before their own eyes, and I got into the carriage alone with Fr. Gury, without human support, and drove back to the hostel of the Sarov monastery.[92]

This testimony had a major impact on the faith of the region. It attests to the ability to recognize authentic faith for healing in a person. When you draw out and identify that faith, then you need to be willing to be a fool for Christ and persevere to a breakthrough.

3 ACQUISITION OF THE HOLY SPIRIT: OVERCOMING PERFORMANCE

There is a close connection between being healed by Jesus and desiring greater transformation from Jesus the healer. The healing of Nicholas Motovilov led him to seek guidance on growing in his spiritual life. New students of the Encounter School of Ministry often tell us that their journey into the school started with a healing that they received.

The healing of Motovilov gave rise to Seraphim's teaching known as "On Acquisition of the Holy Spirit." This teaching paints a full picture of the way in which Seraphim pursued the life and gifts of the Holy Spirit. It provides valuable insights into how Seraphim was able to cultivate such a powerful ministry and how others could experience such transformation.

The teaching begins with Seraphim and Motovilov sitting outside the monastery on a tree stump. Before Motovilov tells Seraphim his needs, Seraphim receives a word of knowledge that Motovilov has been searching for the true aim of the Christian life. The man did not yet understand what the Christian life was really about. Motovilov is stunned:

> I must say here that from the age of twelve this thought had constantly troubled me. I had, in fact, approached many clergy about it; but their answers had not satisfied me. This was not known to the Elder. "But no one," continued Father Seraphim, "has given you a precise answer. They have said to you: 'Go to Church, pray to God, do the commandments of God, do good—that is the aim of the Christian life.' Some were even indignant with you for being occupied with profane curiosity and said to you: 'Do not seek things that are beyond you.' But they did not speak as they should. And now poor Seraphim will explain to you in what this aim really consists."[93]

Motovilov wrote that, in his time, many religious leaders were communicating an approach to Christianity that was ultimately rooted in "performance"—the good things you do for God. According to this mindset, the ultimate value of the Christian life is in its various spiritual

156

practices and in good deeds. Seraphim prophetically identified and responded to this mindset:

> Prayer, fasting, vigil and all other Christian activities, however good they may be in themselves, do not constitute the aim of our Christian life, although they serve as the indispensable means of reaching this end. The true aim of our Christian life consists in the acquisition of the Holy Spirit of God. As for fasts, and vigils, and prayer, and almsgiving, and every good deed done for Christ's sake, they are only means of acquiring the Holy Spirit of God. But mark, my son, only the good deed done for Christ's sake brings us the fruits of the Holy Spirit.[94]

Seraphim recognized that the Holy Spirit is at the center of the Christian life; He makes the encounter with Jesus possible, as He makes Jesus present to us and unites us with the Father. Seraphim recognized that many Christians of his time were caught up in the perfor-

THE TRUE AIM OF OUR CHRISTIAN LIFE CONSISTS IN THE ACQUISITION OF THE HOLY SPIRIT OF GOD.[94]

mance of Christian practices, thinking such engagement would eventually get them into the kingdom of God. But God is not content with our engagement in these practices so that we can get to heaven. Rather we engage in these practices to get the kingdom of God inside of us! Seraphim understood that the kingdom of God can be experienced "on earth as it is in heaven" by receiving the Holy Spirit in our hearts:

And so it must be in actual fact, for the grace of God must dwell within us, in our heart, because the Lord said: The Kingdom of God is within you (Lk. 17:21). By the Kingdom of God the Lord meant the grace of the Holy Spirit. This Kingdom of God is now within us, and the grace of the Holy Spirit shines upon us and warms us from without as well. It fills the surrounding air with many fragrant odours, sweetens our senses with heavenly delight and floods our hearts with unutterable joy. Our present state is that of which the Apostle says, The Kingdom of God is not food and drink, but righteousness and peace and joy in the Holy Spirit (Rom. 14:17). Our faith consists not in the plausible words of earthly wisdom, but in the demonstration of the Spirit and power (1 Cor. 2:4).[95]

Here Seraphim simply echoes the words of Sacred Scripture about the reality of the kingdom of God. If receiving the Holy Spirit gives us access to the kingdom of God, then acquiring a greater share of the Holy Spirit is the ultimate aim of the spiritual life. The key to overcoming a performance mentality is to acknowledge that the life of the Holy Spirit is available now and is a reality that we can receive and experience. When we engage in spiritual practices or works (prayer, fasting, almsgiving, and so on), we should do so with an expectant faith that God will pour out more of His Spirit on us. For Seraphim, there was no limit to "the more" that we can receive of the Holy Spirit.

> BY THE KINGDOM OF GOD THE LORD MEANT THE GRACE OF THE HOLY SPIRIT.[95]

4 ACQUISITION OF THE HOLY SPIRIT: INCREASE IN OUR SPIRITUAL GIFTS

In Matthew chapter 10, Jesus gave his disciples authority to cast out evil spirits and to heal every disease and infirmity. He then commanded them to "make this proclamation: 'The kingdom of heaven is at hand.' Cure the sick, raise the dead, cleanse lepers, drive out demons. Without cost you have received; without cost you are to give" (Matthew 10:7-8).

The last line of this quote is of special importance to us: "without cost you have received; without cost you are to give." What the disciples received from Jesus—the ability to participate in healing and deliverance ministry—they needed to exercise, to give to others.

Seraphim's teaching on the acquisition of the Holy Spirit emphasizes how essential the gifts of the Holy Spirit are in receiving more of the Holy Spirit:

> If we understand the commandments of Christ and of the Apostles aright, our business as Christians consists not in increasing the number of our good deeds, which are only the means of furthering the purpose of our Christian life, but in deriving from them the utmost profit, that is in acquiring the most abundant gifts of the Holy Spirit.[96]

For St. Seraphim, seeking and receiving the gifts of the Holy Spirit was essential to living a full life in the Holy Spirit. It is one thing to receive a spiritual gift, and it is a completely different thing to grow and mature in that gift. Once we receive the gifts of the Holy Spirit, how do we increase their presence and power in our life and ministry?

St. Seraphim compared the increase in the gifts of the Spirit to the spread of fire:

> Distribute the Holy Spirit's gifts of grace to those in need of them, just as a lighted candle burning with earthly fire shines itself and lights other candles for the illumining of all in other places, without diminishing its own light. And if it is so with regard to earthly fire, what shall we say about the fire of the grace of the All-Holy Spirit of God? For earthly riches decrease with distribution, but the more the heavenly riches of God's grace are distributed, the more they increase in him who distributes them.[97]

OUR BUSINESS AS CHRISTIANS CONSISTS IN ACQUIRING THE MOST ABUNDANT GIFTS OF THE HOLY SPIRIT.

Unless a fire spreads, it will go out. But if the fire is shared, not only does it get brighter but its power and heat increase. Seraphim tells us that this should be the way we understand the gifts of the Holy Spirit. We need to spread the gifts we receive in order for them to grow. Using the spiritual gifts that we receive is the same as giving those gifts to others. And our growth in a gift is dependent on our willingness to share what we have received.

At the Encounter School of Ministry, we are invested in the transformation and growth of each student, so that they can demonstrate the Gospel in their sphere of influence. We have created a culture of faith, and our students have opportunities to hear and receive ministry from people who operate in the gifts of the Holy Spirit: in prophetic ministry, healing ministry, power evangelization, and so on. Sometimes we hear students remark about speakers: "Wow, God gave them such a powerful anointing. I definitely could never operate at that level!" Remarks like this reveal an incomplete understanding of the gifts of the Spirit.

These speakers, myself included, often reveal that commitment to continual exercise of a gift in-

> FOR EARTHLY RICHES DECREASE WITH DISTRIBUTION, BUT THE MORE THE HEAVENLY RICHES OF GOD'S GRACE ARE DISTRIBUTED, THE MORE THEY INCREASE IN HIM WHO DISTRIBUTES THEM.

creases its impact in their life and ministry. For example, the gift of prophecy is ordered to hearing God's voice for others, to build up, encourage, and console them (see 1 Corinthians 14:3). Most people who receive the gift of prophecy start exercising it at a pretty basic level. The impact of the gift usually increases as the individual continues to exercise it and build others up with it.

As St. Seraphim taught, growth in the spiritual gifts comes from a continual exercise of them.

5 A REVELATION-BASED MINDSET

How do we access the gifts of the Holy Spirit? St. Seraphim ministered with many of the gifts of the Holy Spirit, during a time and in a place in which spiritual manifestations were not frequent. When he was asked how he did such miraculous ministry for the countless people who came to him, he did not say it was because he possessed a particular charism or great authority in the Holy Spirit. He did not attribute the miracles to his intense devotional life with Jesus. Rather:

> What the Lord tells me as His servant I pass on to those in need of benefit. Like iron to the smith, so I have surrendered myself and my will to the Lord God. As he wills, so I act.[98]

Seraphim's response is so simple and yet so profound! He attributed all his ministry to a total dependence on receiving revelation from the Lord. Once he heard what Jesus wanted him to say or do for the person in need, he obeyed. His obedience to the word of the Lord brought forth the prophetic word, the healing of hearts and bodies, and more.

Seraphim did not invent this principle: it comes straight from Jesus. When the Jewish leaders questioned Him after the healing of a crippled man, Jesus responded: "Very truly, I tell you, the Son can do nothing on his own, but only what he sees the Father doing; for whatever the Father does, the Son does likewise" (John 5:19, NRSVCE).

Jesus shows us that Abba Father instructed Him on how to bring heaven to earth in the ministry moment. Even though the Spirit of the Lord was upon Him and anointed Him to bring healing (see Luke 4:18), the operation of this anointing was guided by the revelation of the Father.

St. Seraphim had a simple and expectant faith that when people came to him with a need, Jesus was ready to reveal what Seraphim should say and do. His role was to carry out Jesus' desire. And he repeatedly saw what Jesus did through his obedience.

In other words, receiving the anointing is insufficient for the supernatural manifestation. The operation of the Spirit's gifts requires the revelation that comes through the prayer connection with the Father. Recognizing our dependence on God for revelation in each action of ministry is essential to growing in our ministry. It also keeps us too from taking credit for any of the good fruit that comes through our ministry.

We could call this the mailman mindset. The mailman receives and delivers the mail. He might give you a package that contains thousands of dollars. If you open the gift in front of him, he could give thanks with you for the gift, but he could not take credit for it. In the same way, we ministers of the Gospel are God's mail carriers. We receive his revelation and deliver what we receive. When a breakthrough comes for someone we are praying for, we cannot take the credit. We thank the Sender, who used us to deliver it.

> RECOGNIZING OUR DEPENDENCE ON GOD FOR REVELATION IN EACH ACTION OF MINISTRY IS ESSENTIAL TO GROWING IN OUR MINISTRY.

In healing ministry, this principle is very important. It is not uncommon for students to receive a revelation of their authority in Christ and proceed to pray in a particular way—say, exclusively with prayers of command. Although this can bear great fruit, praying for healing without seeking how Jesus wants you to pray will always limit the fruit. As we mentioned earlier, Jesus prayed for healing in multiple manners and modes, because he acted in obedience to the Father's guidance in each case.[99]

Jesus did not take any credit for Himself; He directed all the glory to the Father.

Just as He submitted completely to the revelation of His Father, we need to depend completely on the revelation of Jesus to us through the Holy Spirit. When we embrace this and acknowledge our dependence, miracles as well as humility are natural fruits.

St. Seraphim, pray for us!

CONCLUSION
A PROPHETIC PERSPECTIVE

*Have great confidence and faith to receive and minister
by the transforming power of the Holy Spirit*

Jesus Christ is alive! He has not stopped manifesting his supernatural love through the power of the Holy Spirit working through His people. Now that we have completed this journey of receiving inspiration and ministry lessons from these holy saints, I hope it is clear that the life and gifts of the Holy Spirit have been evident throughout our two-thousand-plus-year history of advancing the kingdom of God. We can look to Spirit-filled saints who have gone before us for faith, wisdom, and practical guidance. I pray that you experience some of the incredible fruit that I have from learning from these saints' lives and ministries.

As we read about the amazing exploits and the demonstrations of power that happened at the hands of the saints, it's all too easy to put them on a pedestal. Yes, God chose St. Vincent Ferrer to preach repentance and release signs, wonders, and miracles to revive a morally corrupt European Church hundreds of years ago. Entire nations and continents still need revival now, but God did not call St. Vincent to this age. He is calling us.

God chose St. Philip Neri to be a leader in re-evangelizing the city of Rome one person at a time, through joy and the power of the Holy Spirit. Our cities too need to be re-evangelized, but God did not call St. Philip Neri to this today. He is calling us.

God chose St. Catherine of Siena for a life of intimacy and world-changing supernatural ministry in a male-dominated culture. The Church still needs the grace and influence that God has given to women. The Church desperately needs the daughters and sons of our Father to rise up and boldly advance the kingdom. The God who called St. Catherine then is calling you today.

God chose St. Francis Xavier to go to nations that had never heard the Gospel, and Francis' supernatural ministry brought countless souls into the kingdom. There are still nations and peoples that have not received the Gospel. God is calling you to reach the unreached.

God chose St. Padre Pio and St. Seraphim out of their hidden lives to shine as bright lights of grace and power, bringing countless Christians supernatural ministry and building up the Church through their prayer. There is still a great need for spiritual lighthouses, for homes where the people of God can receive life-changing ministry. God did not call Padre Pio and Seraphim to this today. He is calling us.

Jesus lived a supernatural life of proclaiming and demonstrating the kingdom of God. These saints did the same thing in their time. God has called and chosen us to be His supernatural saints right now.

As you step into God's call to demonstrate His love in your sphere of influence, I want to offer some perspectives that I believe God wants us to have.

PROPHETIC PERSPECTIVE

Toward the end of the twentieth century, Pope St. John Paul II publicly called for the Church to engage in a New Evangelization. He wrote:

> I sense that the moment has come to commit all of the Church's energies to a new evangelization and to the mission *ad gentes*. No believer in Christ, no institution of the Church can avoid this supreme duty: to proclaim Christ to all peoples.[100]

Pope Benedict XVI publicly prayed for a New Pentecost. In a homily at St. Patrick's Cathedral in New York City, he prayed:

> [L]et us implore from God the grace of a new Pentecost for the Church in America. May tongues of fire, combining burning love of God and neighbor with zeal for the spread of Christ's Kingdom, descend on all present![101]

Pope Francis has continued the emphasis on praying for a New Pentecost. In the first year of his pontificate, he said:

> We need to pray for a New Pentecost for the Church in this hour! . . . The Church needs to rise up in this hour with the same power with which she transformed the world of the first centuries. She can—by the power of the Holy Spirit![102]

The Holy Spirit has led the Church to invest all our energy in the New Evangelization. The popes know that the first evangelization was only possible through the power of the Holy Spirit, who was poured out on the early Church at Pentecost. The life and gifts of the Holy Spirit enabled the early Church to proclaim and supernaturally demonstrate the Gospel, to turn the world upside down (see Acts 17:6). We need the same outpouring.

As we are invited to pray for a New Pentecost to fuel the New Evangelization, we should have great confidence and faith to receive and minister by the transforming power of the Holy Spirit. In many places, the Church is already seeing signs of the Holy Spirit's outpouring. The New Pentecost is taking effect.

For many faithful Christians, the outpouring of the

life and gifts of the Holy Spirit is uncomfortable. Fortunately, Jesus revealed that the Holy Spirit is the Advocate, a role that includes comforting (see John 14:26). We need to get beyond any hang-ups that we have about the New Pentecost flowing into the Church. Then we can help others be positioned to receive the outpouring of the Spirit, so they too can be empowered.

EARLY AND LATE OUTPOURINGS

I believe that there could be a greater significance to what the Holy Spirit wants in this age, the New Pentecost, than the first Pentecost. When we come to understand this current season in God's plan, we can be more intentional and bear greater fruit for Jesus' harvest of souls.

Let's look at the first Pentecost. Directly after the disciples received the outpouring of the Holy Spirit on that day, those observing their behavior were amazed, confused, astonished, and bewildered. Some concluded that the 120 disciples had to be drunk on new wine (see Acts 2:5-13). Peter responded:

> These people are not drunk, as you suppose, for it is only nine o'clock in the morning. No, this is what was spoken through the prophet Joel:
>
> "It will come to pass in the last days," God says,
> "that I will pour out a portion of my spirit upon all flesh. Your sons and your daughters shall prophesy,
> your young men shall see visions,
> your old men shall dream dreams.
> Indeed, upon my servants and my handmaids
> I will pour out a portion of my spirit in those days,
> and they shall prophesy. (Acts 2:15-18)

Peter connected this first Pentecost outpouring to the prophecy in Joel 3:1.Five verses before that prophecy, Joel described what the outpouring of the Spirit would look like:

> Children of Zion, delight and rejoice in the LORD, your God! For he has faithfully given you the early rain, sending rain down on you,
> the early and the late rains as before. (Joel 2:23)

Joel set the coming of the Spirit within the context of God sending an early rain and a late rain. These are references to the two major rain seasons of Israel in the course of planting and harvesting their crops.

In the spring, there would be an early rain season, *yoreh* in Hebrew . At this time the Israelites would plant their seed, and *yoreh* was needed to establish the crop and start the necessary process of growth. Before the harvest, they would receive a late rain, called in Hebrew the *malkosh*. This rain was much heavier than the early rain. It signified the end of the growing season, and it prepared the soil for the coming harvest.[103]

It could well be that the first Pentecost was the promised early rain, the Holy Spirit being poured out for the initial growth, the explosion of the kingdom. The New Pentecost that we are now praying for and starting to receive could be a fulfillment of the *malkosh*, the late rain being poured out to prepare for the harvest. In interpreting the parable of the weeds in the field, Jesus compared His second coming to a harvest: "The harvest is the end of the age, and the harvesters are angels" (Matthew 13:39).

Even though Jesus informed us that we will know neither the day nor the hour of His second coming (see Matthew 25:13), He spent a considerable amount of time informing us of general signs. And though the Church has always rejected attempts to provide specific timelines about His second coming, she has been open to prophetic revelation about it. For the prophet Amos notes that "the Lord God does nothing without revealing his plan to his servants the prophets" (Amos 3:7).

I believe one of the most trusted prophetic sources about Jesus' second coming is St. Faustina Kowalska.

In her diary, *Divine Mercy in My Soul*, St. Faustina received and wrote down revelation from Jesus in the early 20th century. In this prophetic revelation Jesus communicated the immense depth of His mercy, His desire for souls to approach Him with repentance for sin, and His longing to transform lives with His forgiveness and grace. Jesus spoke to Faustina about a coming age of Divine Mercy that would sweep the earth and lead countless sinners to conversion. In the revelation she received, Jesus spoke to Faustina on many occasions about His second coming. For example:

(1) Speak to the world about My mercy; let all mankind recognize My unfathomable mercy. It is a sign for the end times; after it will come the day of justice. While there is still time, let them have recourse to the fount of My mercy; let them profit from the Blood and Water which gushed forth for them. (*Diary*, 848; see John 19:34)

(2) Write this: before I come as the Just Judge, I am coming first as the King of Mercy. (*Diary*, 83)

(3) I am prolonging the time of mercy for the sake of sinners. But woe to them if they do not recognize this time of My visitation. My daughter, secretary of My mercy, your duty is not only to write about

and proclaim My mercy, but also to beg for this grace for them, so that they too may glorify My mercy. (*Diary*, 1160)[104]

St. Faustina's revelations are considered private ones, and thus Catholics are not required to believe them. But if they are authentic, this time of mercy could be like the late rain of the Holy Spirit preparing for the harvest, the second coming of Jesus. I see an intimate connection here with what God is doing in the outpouring of the New Pentecost to fuel our New Evangelization. The Spirit is providing supernatural instruments to bring God's mercy to a sinful world.

If it is true that the age of the Divine Mercy and the New Pentecost is a fulfillment of the late rain before the harvest, then we need to approach the work of evangelization with great urgency. We need the mindset of Jesus as He looked out over the crowds and stated that the harvest was abundant (see Matthew 9:37-38). We need to see the world around us as ripe for His harvest of salvation from sin and death.

WHAT THIS MEANS FOR US

I believe that right now is an exciting time for a Christian to be alive. Why is this time exciting? Because "where sin increased, grace overflowed all the more" (Romans 5:20). We can expect God's grace to overflow in us right now. Whenever his grace overflows, things happen!

The darker the night sky gets, the brighter the stars shine. Right now God is inviting us to be the stars that shine in the midst of a corrupt generation (see Philippians 2:15). We are called to proclaim the Gospel and demonstrate it with the supernatural signs of God's power and love.

St. Paul teaches that when Jesus ascended to heaven, he gave gifts to the Church: apostles, prophets, evangelists, pastors, and teachers, "to equip the holy ones for the work of ministry, for building up the body of Christ" (Ephesians 4:12). Paul shows that we don't start off fully equipped. Although this book has provided amazing testimonies and ministry lessons to help you grow in your ministry, in no way can knowledge alone provide the kind of training and formation that we need to grow in the gifts and power of the Holy Spirit.

Discipleship—defined as students following teachers and growing in greater maturity and fruitfulness under their guidance—is the mode Jesus set for growing in supernatural ministry. The discipleship that He gave defines the kind of environment that we need in order to grow. He taught and modeled what ministry looks like, expecting his followers to do what He did. He encouraged them, held them accountable, and provided correction when needed. Discipleship is more than a matter of having the right knowledge.

We need to receive training for the work of ministry, so that we can build up the body of Christ and advance the kingdom of God in our time and sphere of influence. As new movements and ministries emerge to answer the call to equip the people of God for ministry, we can draw from the richness of our Catholic heritage and the witness of the saints. The world needs powerful sons and daughters of God proclaiming and demonstrating the kingdom of God.

We can be greatly consoled knowing that God has led us into this time of New Pentecost and New Evangelization with the example of our older brothers and sisters, who have modeled lifestyles of holy power and holy purity. Not only can we be assured of their solid witness to us, but we can know that they are interceding for us. They will help us become the powerful Church that Jesus died for!

All you holy saints, pray for us!

ENCOUNTER
SCHOOL OF MINISTRY

Drawing from the richness of our Catholic heritage, we seek to teach, equip, and activate disciples to demonstrate the love of God through the power of the Holy Spirit in their sphere of influence.

Learn more at **encounterschool.org**.

INDEX

1 Throughout this book, I utilize the term "supernatural ministry" as opposed to "charismatic ministry" or "divine power ministry." My usage is based on the distinction made by St. Thomas Aquinas. He used the term "supernatural" to describe demonstrations of God's love through humans that are beyond the natural order. For greater insight, please refer to Andrew Murray's paper "The Spiritual and the Supernatural according to Thomas Aquinas," delivered at the Biennial Conference in Philosophy, Religion and Culture, Catholic Institute of Sydney, October 3-4, 1998, https://www.cis.catholic.edu.au/Files/Murray-SpiritualSupernatural.pdf.

2 See encounterschool.org/approvals.

3 Pope Benedict XVI, Homily on the Solemnity of All Saints. Vatican Basilica, November 1, 2006,, vatican.va/content/benedict-xvi/en/homilies/2006/documents/hf_ben-xvi_hom_20061101_all-saints.html.

4 Andrew Pradel, OP, *St. Vincent Ferrer: Angel of the Judgement,* trans. T. A. Dixon, OP (Charlotte, NC: TAN Books, 2000), 48-49.

5 Bishop Pietro Ranzano, *Life of Vincent Ferrer.* 1455-1456, trans. Andrew Pradel.

6 The record of this dream is a letter that St. Vincent wrote to Benedict XIII.

7 For example, you can read the following to learn more about his approach to the interior senses at: St. Thomas Aquinas. Summa Theologica. Part 1, Question 78, Article 4

8 Pradel, Chapter 5.

9 See Amanda Ruggeri, "Do we really live longer than our ancestors?" *BBC Future*, October 2, 2018.

10 James Strong, *Strong's Exhaustive Concordance of the Bible* (London: Abingdon Press, 1890).

11 Pradel, Chap. 6.

12 St. Vincent Ferrer, "How to Preach," in *Treatise on the Spiritual Life* (Vatican: Pontifical University Saint Thomas Aquinas, April 5, 2001), vatican.va /spirit/documents/spirit_20010405_vincenzo-ferrer_en.html.

13 *Ibid.*

14 Pradel, chap. 6.

15 *ibid*

16 Pradel,, chap. 14.

17 *ibid*

18 *Ex opere operato,* a Latin expression meaning "by the work worked," refers to the fact that the sacraments confer grace when the sign is validly effected, not as the result of activity on the part of the recipient but by the power and promise of God.

19 Steve Cunningham, "St Vincent Ferrer the Angel of the Apocalypse," *Sensus Fidelium* Presentation], McAdenville, NC, April 5, 2014.

20 For example: Testimony from Fr. Ignatius Manfredonia: "While listening to the Encounter program while driving, I heard you call out on the show anyone out there with pain in the left knee and it took me a moment to realize, "Hey, I have pain in the left knee!" I placed my hand on my knee and prayed with you, you said the prayer of adjuration and I thought I felt some warmth in my knee, but I definitely had a sense that I had been healed and experienced joy…I tested my knee by doing some movements that normally would cause pain and there was none. It also felt strong while walking. For the next few days after that, I was always

amazed that my knee didn't hurt when doing those movements that would usually cause pain and I would say to myself, "It really is healed."

21 Note that the earliest accounts from Gallonio and Bacci confirm these manifestations.

22 Rev Pietro Giacomo Bacci, *The Life of St. Philip Neri Apostle of Rome,* trans. F. A. Faber (London: Thomas Richardson and Son, 1902), bk. 3, chap. 4.

23 *99 Catholics. (2021, June 17). Release of Demons | by Saint Philip Neri. Polk Township, MO United States.* Story also recounted in *Bacci* Bk 3, Chap. 10.

24 *ibid*

25 Bacci, bk. 5, chap. 2.

26 Rev Antonia Gallonio, *The Life of St. Philip Neri,* trans. Jerome Betram (San Francisco, CA: Ignatius Press, 2005), Chapter 3

27 *ibid.*

28 Bacci, bk. 2, chap. 3.

29 *ibid*

30 *ibid*

31 Gallonio recounts six testimonies of this nature, and Bacci recounts one.

32 Gallonio, chap. 11.

33 Bacci, bk 5, chap. 4.

34 Gallonio, chap. 8, section 91.

35 Bacci bk. 5 chap. 3.

36 *ibid*

37 Bacci, bk. 5, chap. 4.

38 Ibid.

39 Bacci. bk. 3, chap. 3.

40 Gallonio, para. 224.

41 Roper, Dr. Gregory. (2012, November 30). *Fool for Love: St. Philip Neri and the Reform of Rome.* [University of Dallas]. Dallas, TX United States.

42 Sigrid Undset, *Catherine of Siena* (San Francisco: Ignatius Press, 2009), p. 52.

43 *Undset, p 58.*

44 Raymond of Capua, *Life of St. Catherine of Siena* (Washington: TAN Books, 2011), 220.

45 Undset, p. 145.

46 Raymond of Capua, 220.

47 Raymond of Capua, 220-221.

48 For a fuller understanding of the distinction between the Rite of Exorcism and simple deliverance ministry, see Chapters 3 and 4 in the book *Deliverance Ministry*, published by the International Doctrinal Commission of CHARIS.

49 *The responses are found in the Charism FAQs at encounterministries.us.*

50 Raymond of Capua, 216.

51 Raymond of Capua p. 220

52 Raymond of Capua, 222.

53 Raymond of Capua, 223.

54 Undset, p. 146.

55 Vatican Council II, *Lumen Gentium* [Dogmatic Constitution on the Church], 12, www.vatican.va/archive/hist_councils/ii_vatican_council/documents/vat-ii_const_19641121_lumen-gentium_en.html.

56 Undset, p. 119.

57 Raymond of Capua, 183.
58 Undset chap. 9.
59 Raymond of Capua, 199.
60 Raymond of Capua, 200.
61 Raymond of Capua, 195.
62 *Ibid.*
63 *Raymond of Capua p. 197.*
64 Undset, 210.
65 St. Francis Xavier, *The Life and Letters of St. Francis Xavier,* trans. Henry James Coleridge, new ed. (London: Burns and Oates, 1881), 115.
66 Xavier, p. 72.
67 Xavier, p. 112.
68 Francis Xavier, p. 116.
69 Francis Xavier, p. 119.
70 His Japanese name was Han-Sir. It is unclear why he was initially known to the Portuguese as Anger.
71 Francis Xavier *p. 312.*
72 Francis Xavier *p. 313.*
73 Francis Xavier *p. 510.*
74 Francis Xavier, p. 117.
75 *ibid*
76 Official Canonization of Padre Pio, June 16, 2002, vatican.va/news_service/liturgy/saints/ns_lit_doc_s00s0616.paredre_pio_en.html.
77 Vatican's Summary of Padre Pio's Life. https://www.vatican.va/news_services/liturgy/saints/ns_lit_doc_20020616_padre-pio_en.html
78 James Strong, Strong's Exhaustive Concordance of the Bible (London: Abingdon Press, 1890).
79 St. John Chrysostom, *Homilies on Hebrews,* Homily 3, in *Nicene and Post-Nicene Fathers,* First Series, vol. 14, Philip Schaff, ed. (Buffalo, NY: Christian Literature Publishing, 1889).
80 *Letters* I, no. 141.
81 Fr. Alessio Parent, *"Send Me Your Guardian Angel": Padre Pio,* 4th ed. (1983), chap. 7.
82 Padre Pio da Pietrelcina, *EPISTOLARIO, II: Correspondence with the Noblewoman Raffaelina Cerase 1914-1915* (National Centre for Padre Pio), Letter 64, 403-404.
83 Kevin O'Brien, *The Ignatian Adventure: Experiencing the Spiritual Exercises of St. Ignatius in Daily Life* (Chicago, IL: Loyola Press, 2011), p. 95.
84 Fr. Alessio Parente, OFM Cap., *"Send Me Your Guardian Angel": Padre Pio* 4th ed. (publisher unknown, 1984), chap. 3.
85 Parente, *chap. 3.* Note that at times Padre Pio called his angel "little child," an Italian term of affection.

86 Congregation for Divine Worship and the Discipline of the Sacraments, *Directory on Popular Piety and the Liturgy: Principles and Guidelines* (Vatican City, 2001), no. 127.
87 Padre Pio da Pietrelcina, *EPISTOLARIO, II: Correspondence with the Noblewoman Raffaelina Cerase* 1914-1915, Letter 64 (National Center for Padre Pio), 403-404.
88 Archimandrite Lazarus Moore, *An Extraordinary Peace: St. Seraphim, Flame of Sarov* (Port Townsend, WA: Anaphora Press, 2009), 234.
89 See Moore, p. 91.
90 Moore, 237.

[91] Moore, 238.

[92] Moore, 245-247.

[93] St. Seraphim of Sarov, *On Acquisition of the Holy Spirit* (Monee, IL: CreateSpace, 2014), 8-9.

[94] Seraphim, 9.

[95] *ibid.*

[96] Seraphim, 28.

[97] Seraphim, 30.

[98] Seraphim *p 233.*

[99] See the section "Understanding Healing Ministry" in chapter 2.

[100] Pope John Paul II, *Redemptoris Missio* [Encyclical on the Church's Missionary Mandate], 3, vatican.va/content/john-paul-ii/en/encyclicals/documents/hf_jp-ii_enc_07121990_redemptoris-missio.html.

[101] Pope Benedict XVI, Homily at St. Patrick's Cathedral, April 19, 2008, vatican.va/content/benedict-xvi/en/homilies/2008/documents/hf_ben-xvi_hom_20080419_st-patrick-ny.html.

[102] Pope Francis, quoted in Tom Hoopes, "This Sunday, Start the New Pentecost for America," Ex Corde at Benedictine College, May 28, 2020, https://excorde.org/2020/this-sunday-start-the-new-pentecost-for-america.

[103] See Rabbi Reuven Chaim Klein's exposition of the concept of early and late rains in Old Testament context in his article "Rain, Rain, Come Again," *What's in a Word?* Ohr Somayach International. Jerusalem, Israel.

[104] Quotes taken from St. Faustina Kowalska, *Diary: Divine Mercy in My Soul* (Stockbridge, MA: Marian Press. 2005). Numbers refer to paragraphs in the *Diary*.

Made in the USA
Middletown, DE
16 October 2023

40693676R00113